Journey to Destiny,
Traveling Through
Infertility

Danielle Q. Kinsey

iUniverse, Inc.
Bloomington

Journey to Destiny, Traveling Through Infertility

iUniverse books may be ordered through booksellers or by contacting:

iUniverse
1663 Liberty Drive
Bloomington, IN 47403
www.iuniverse.com
1-800-Authors (1-800-288-4677)

ISBN: 978-1-4620-3539-7 (sc)
ISBN: 978-1-4620-3540-3 (ebk)

Printed in the United States of America

iUniverse rev. date: 12/22/2011

This book is dedicated to my Destiny
and to yours

Acknowledgements

There has been so much inspiration, selfless acts, and beautiful people that have helped me shape the concept of this labor of love. First, I have to acknowledge Jesus Christ for even acquainting me with this powerful journey and allowing me to share my experiences. God has blessed me with my wonderful husband, Deon Kinsey. He is the foundation of my heart's joy and he has loved me through so many of my personal challenges. He has walked right beside me throughout this journey; feeling every hurt, devastation, and triumph. I love him endlessly. I would like to thank my parents, William and June Tyler for sacrificing their entire life to help fulfill my dreams. My mother is the reason why I write. Her encouragement is the reason why my confidence and imagination knows no limitation. I'm still in love with my parents as if I was a newborn depending on their nurture. My family is a vital piece of me; I want to thank the Tyler/Anderson/Kinsey/Jeffries/Boddie families for their unwavering support. I have three incredible cousins, Whitney Bonds, Lindsey Turner, and Brittany Washington who are my true sisters. Our sisterhood has helped shaped the woman I am today and I am so glad that our friendships has stood the test of grace! Whitney, you are my sister; the one that allows me to be my entire self. True friendship is something that most people do not get a chance to grasp, so I am blessed to have it. I want to thank Laura Jeffries, Tshona Johnson, Jacqueline Woods, Kellie Williams, and Renee Hollis for their friendship. I adore the pure bliss that your love affords me. I have to acknowledge the professional team who helped my dreams of being a published author a reality. That team included the iUniverse Publishing Team, Patria Dunn-Rowe, and Marcella Richardson. I want to thank the two tiny souls who have made the journey through infertility worth every minute. I love you endlessly and unconditionally. My life is yours. Last, but least; I thank everyone who have took the time to exist inside of my words. God bless you.

Truth

I cannot deny
That sometimes
I could revisit that scared little girl that lives inside of me
The little girl, who was created by abuse
Who moves through life with anxiety and indecision
Who views herself through the heartless opinions
Of people who wish her violence
Reverting back to her will allow me to live in the fear that
Keeps her trapped inside of my body
So that I could remain silent and my thoughts sit in
peace
But I must shuffle through these feelings now
That seems impossible to confront
And it is with great clumsiness and fretfulness that I
confront them
I am falling all over my emotions
I continue to resist the truth
I will run from the pain and everything that it wants to
show me
I will run from freedom because bondage is really where
I want to be
I have found a home in this confinement
Now I'm staring change into its eyes
It must be a savage, because it's merciless, its threatens
to kill every coping mechanism that has allowed me to
ignore this pain
I am afraid

Afraid of these feelings and now my heart is pleading
Pleading that the reality is gentler than expected
Because this is the only way out of the wreckage
This is the only way to calm the heavy panting of my
breath
You are in my reach
I see you so vividly
The finish line is running towards me
Full speed ahead
And once my foot has touched the other side of it
Truth, I know you are waiting for me with arms wide open
With eyes so welcoming
With intentions to heal the broken pieces of my heart

Truth

A wise person once said, "There is no agony like an untold story inside of you". That's why it is so important for me to tell the story that is inside of me. I have accepted that the only way to ease the pain in my heart is to tell my truth. When I first came upon that philosophical and penetrating statement, tears flooded my eyes. I finally felt free from the manipulation and fear of thinking that I was not good enough to courageously share my story. For so long, I allowed anxiety to paralyze me and shut my mouth. I allowed it to convince me to silence and to own the thoughts of being too insecure, uneducated, and insufficient to share my truth with the world. It gave me the confidence I needed to make myself transparent so that people would see my authenticity, free from pretense and distraction. I pray that my words and experiences can be the visual to help guide people through their own struggles. God has given me such a powerful testimony through experiencing infertility, and I refuse to let that story be trapped inside of me any longer.

This is not a step-by-step guide to getting pregnant, although I will literally navigate you through my journey to get there. I pray that this book serves as a bit of relief, comfort, and inspiration to the women whose hearts break on a daily basis, whose tears saturate their pillows every night because their journey to motherhood seems endless and impossible. Most importantly, this is for every woman who has ever had to experience anything so traumatic, that it threatened to destroy everything that they are or have the potential to be.

Take this journey with me and by the conclusion of this love letter to the desiring mother; all women, I pray you find yourself sprinting towards your finish line.

Truth is a proven sincerity, honesty, and righteousness.

(John 8:32) "And he shall know the truth: and the truth shall set you free"

The journey towards my destiny has been an incredible, tragic, heartbreaking, beautiful, miraculous and ultimately necessary trial. The progress that I've made through this learning experience is remarkable, but that process didn't come without devastation, and facing my own self. This journey didn't come without disappointment, faces of pity, and days that left me in total ruins. Through sharing the experiences from my life, I want to serve as a voice for women all over the world, who have gone through humiliation, isolation, and depression as a result of infertility. At one time or another during this journey, those three things have outlined it all. Humiliation for being a woman, who could not carry a baby, was more than overwhelming and painful. I couldn't understand why I wasn't allowed to do something so natural and destined. God gave women one of the most beautiful, and most vital capacities mankind could ever have; to be the vehicle that helps assists him in bringing life into this world. Here I am . . . unable to take part in that truth; Here you are, unable to take part in that truth. I know it doesn't seem fair or just, because I felt the same way, and that's why I want to invite you to come close, and exist inside of this story about God's love, grace, compassion, discipline, and mercy.

The isolation that I felt in my experience is one of the main reasons I wanted to open my life up to the world and share what I've gone through, I want to touch the hearts of the women who have to suffer at the hands of infertility. Isolation was one of the feelings that were most potent, and loud in my journey. I actually felt alone, trapped in this teeny tiny box that defined me as a woman, with no one to free or comfort me. I think it was easier to separate myself from the world around me because of the embarrassment of the infertility. I felt alone because no one around me was experiencing it. So, who was I to reach out to without feeling alienated because of my struggle? But how much longer can we treat a topic that is all too common like it is taboo? Even though people in the public eye have made fair attempts to acknowledge their experience with infertility; the voice of the common woman has gone unheard and unacknowledged. Part of that problem is because we as common women have put this ban on infertility, resulting in us creating an emotional and mental aversion to the issue. I want to own the voice of the common woman. I want to speak for the woman, who is simple, yet strategic in her ways. The woman, who has great ambition with minimal resources, but still manages to succeed. I represent the woman, who hides behind her efforts and smile, because she can not hide behind luxury and material treasures. The average Mary Jane, who strenuously work to just survive, let alone afford the cost of infertility options. I want to own that voice. The voice, that is not ashamed of destroying the ban of embarrassment

Through my journey of infertility, I felt no one understood, because they didn't have to walk in my shoes, and live inside my head. They didn't know of this pain that paralyzed ever fiber of my being. Now that I have made it through, I feel that my story can touch the lives of women, who are currently going through or have been through the same thing, and they will appreciate my message, as well as learn from it. The solitude alone killed me and the lack of another's human compassion merely destroyed my self importance, but I pray my story will give you the compassion and support you need to follow this journey until it ends. I want you to know that you are important enough for someone to step outside of their own circumstances to walk with you through your own. Although this journey is talking about my experiences with infertility; this story is so much more than that. It is a story about redemption, allowing God to take the mess that I've made out of myself and my life to turn it into a beautiful portrait that still has grooves to fill. I want to share with you how experiencing infertility unraveled insecurity and past experience that has caused trauma in my life. It caused me to face demons that I wanted to keep buried. With this testimony of infertility and personal tragedy, I want to help other women start to paint their own perfect picture. And no, I don't mean perfect without blemish, I mean brutal honesty. The type of truth that hurts, but is necessary to achieve any type of breakthrough or change. This book is an honest picture that details every pain, hurt, and triumph that paved my path to motherhood. I want you to feel every touch of sorrow that leveled me as low as the ground; every disappointment that left me feeling like living death, and every triumph that picked my determination back up to continue to my destiny. I want you to feel every emotion as if you were me, because you are me. Every woman, whether it be infertility, failed relationships, broken marriages, drug addiction, faith, sexual exploitation, mental instability, or any type of tragedy—has had these same feelings. The feelings of emptiness and hopelessness. The feelings of loneliness and mental anguish, that keep your thoughts and spirits bounded. We all may not share the details, but we all share a similar generalization.

Chapter One

The Little Girl In Me Takes Center Stage

Cruelty

Pain had little meaning until it exploded within my chest
The sudden violence left its fragments lying directly on
my heart
And it hurts
It stings
I feel my skin pulsating
The hurt is separating me from any sanity that I knew
It stirs up emotions that I never knew existed
It's messy
It's bloody
It smears its content all over my soul
Its protrudes out of my internal and stains my clothes
It delivers me into a darkness that I never knew
Darkness so concentrated
That I get lost in the density
And the taste leaves my face colored with intensity
Pain had little meaning before, until it exploded in my
chest
The sudden violence left its fragments on my heart

(Deuteronomy 32:4)
"He is the rock, his work is perfect: for all his ways are judgments: a God of truth and without iniquity, just and right is he". KJV

I can strikingly remember the raw emotion that I felt at the beginning leg of my journey to motherhood. I felt juvenile in my reactions, thoughts, and decisions. What I mean by being childlike in my actions was by owning an immature and close-minded mentality with the situation. I believed that my confrontation with infertility was an unfair punishment from God. I refused to look deeper into his reasoning with allowing me to come face to face with infertility. I just wanted to believe that there was an easy solution to the problem or that it would go away in time. Similar to a little girl whining and tugging at the leg of her daddy; I questioned God repeatedly in the same manner. I wanted to know why I could not get my hands on the prize possession; which was a pregnancy. Exhibiting childlike simplicity, I would literally throw tantrums in the form of tears and screams. I wanted him to know just how miserable and confused I was in my unsuccessful quest to motherhood. My husband and I were doing everything in our power to get pregnant, but nothing worked. So, in true childish form, we adopted a curiosity that threw us in a world that we were not emotionally equipped for: not quite yet.

My husband and I jumped right on in the world of infertility with total ignorance. We started to take heave to all the advice we could garner from the internet, magazines, books, and people. I quickly became an expert on ovulation, with learning how to track the most optical time in my menstrual cycle to get pregnant. I brought ovulation kits from the drug store; in conjunction with using a thermometer to track my temperature. Basically, you take your temperature every morning when you first wake up. You then chart your temperatures and when your temperature starts to elevate; you hit the jackpot. That means that ovulation is near and it's time to have sex with your partner. I would practically stand on my head, to give my husband's sperm the gift of gravity in hopes that it would reach my egg. If, you think that was hard work, we had a ritual to even get to the actual baby-making sex. I daily shoved a dozen of vitamins and herbs down my throat to boost my fertility. I exercised fours times a week and avoided caffeine, alcohol, and fatty foods in my diet. My husband also took part in taking recommendations to boost his fertility, he religiously drunk a concoction of pure honey, raw eggs, and milk to strengthen his sperm count. Our dewy-eyed innocence of wanting to start a family was becoming an obsession, instead of our dream. I started to become so depleted; but my determination to get my hands on my prize possession would not die. The little girl in me was sitting alone and confused in the corner. I felt as though I was being scolded and equalized my inability to conceive as a punishment from God. I actually felt that God was being violent towards me because I took an emotional and mental beating on a daily basis. I felt like this "thing" I was going through, was getting the best of me. All the strength I thought I had became a distant memory, and every day the details of that memory faded farther and farther away. I refer to infertility as "thing" because in this part of my journey, I couldn't acknowledge that I actually had an issue with having a baby. I felt that if I didn't say it, then it didn't exist. It was just another way to psyche myself out of the harsh reality of not being able to get pregnant and another example of my childlike mentality at the time. It was a way to escape the pain and embarrassment of it all. I felt that if I made the problem seem smaller than it really was—by reducing it down to "a thing"—its presence would be less noticeable and intense. The truth was its presence was far from diluted; it was concentrated and deep. It was huge . . . And I felt it everyday . . . all day.

So, this "thing" just kept biting away at my patience, and all I could do was just trying and find a way to lessen the pain of those blows that whooped my backside day in and day out. Everything felt like a personal thrashing: getting a negative pregnancy test, hearing that someone else was pregnant, watching television programs about babies, doctor appointments for fertility testing, and of course the every present thought that I would always be childless. At the time, I truly felt like God had abandoned my despair. The little girl in me felt that her Father left her alone in time out without an explanation. The little girl in me prepared to take center stage and I was ready to get this performance started. I walked up to the microphone and nothing was going to stop the show. My husband and I started actively pursing desperate measures and began discovering more abrasive options. I was confident that I'd finally found the cushioning I needed to ease those backside spankings. Just like bright-eyed kids, we believed our new endeavors would bring us closer to our goals. It was only a matter of time before our lives would be interrupted with midnight feedings; diapers, and coos!

As time went on, needless to say there were no feedings, diapers, or coos . . . only more frustration and impatience. My journey intensified from hormone treatments of pills of Clomid to IUIs. Clomid was a pill that triggered ovulation and help the woman to produce more eggs. The more eggs that are produced, give a greater chance of your partner's sperm to meet a mate. The Clomid therapy proved to be a waste of time because we still had no pregnancy. So without hesitation; we moved to the IUI procedure. IUI is the term used for intrauterine insemination. It is when the woman's partner's sperm is medically placed inside of her during ovulation. The transition of taking pills, going to the doctor's office every other day, to monitor my hormone stimulation and levels, was no easy task. Imagine being emotionally weary, and also having to walk into a doctor's office first thing in the morning, only to be greeted by a medical team who viewed you as just another number. They only care about the statistics of your situation, when your heart, mind, body and soul are wrapped, tied and tangled up in the emotions of it all. I'd thought having a baby was special and intimate, but nothing is intimate about the robotic routine of fertility treatments. I can recall being so devastated when my first insemination with my husband's sperm was a failure. The doctor's initially under stimulated me, only giving me minimal hormone stimulation because of my age, I was only 21. I didn't produce many eggs as a result, leaving it highly unlikely for my husband's sperm to meet a mate. Well, I remember being above and beyond let down, but the worse was our doctor's nonchalant attitude towards the situation. The reasoning for his actions flew so easily and care free out of his mouth, while I had to pick my heart's dream off the floor. I couldn't welcome his nonchalant behavior; all I could think about was the time, money, and emotions that were heavily invested in that one procedure. I started to feel depressed and became almost mute in a sense, which allowed me to feel even more justified in the immaturity of my thoughts. The little girl in me was trying to rationalize the failure of our attempt with the infertility treatment. I went in total tantrum mode; kicking and flinging my arms wildly. I was a 21-year-old married, woman; who walks the straight and narrow path, and I was having so many problems as if I were doing something wrong to warrant this punishment. In my eyes, I was a picture of human perfection. I was responsible, I went to church—including bible study-, studied the word on my own, prayed constantly, fasted, helped others, went to work everyday, took care of my husband, and helped my parents, family, and friends. I was a moderate day super woman! I was unselfish in all my ways, and dedicated my life to serving people; yet God had the nerve, no, the audacity to project so much pain in my life? All I wanted was a baby, someone to call my own, and mold. I wanted someone, who I could cuddle, teach, and kiss; that would love me more than anyone else. Just thinking about how my baby would extend their little arms to reach out for me would take me to a place so soothing I started to crave that feeling. I could almost feel that baby reaching for me because it wants the affection and love that a mother could only give. I found myself sitting in bliss and peace, thoughts like that absorbing my senses until the sharpness of truth cut through it all. The truth was that I wasn't pregnant, and it looked like I would never get there. I could not understand why God was keeping such a blessing from me; a good, well rounded, Christian person.

Wow, looking back in hindsight on my truth, and how I felt at the time, makes me feel frivolous to think that I was "above" the struggles of life or just didn't deserve this heartbreaking and strenuous fight. How could I be so "deserving" and still be without? I actually thought I was "picture perfect"; but the truth was it was only a picture. Behind the images that I choose for people to see, was dirt and vile. Like everyone else, I possessed things that were unflattering to my image, but I tricked myself in thinking That I was really that "picture perfect" image I projected to the world. I actually thought that I deserved what I wanted when I wanted it, and God owed me this baby because of my willingness to live the right way, and be a decent person. I mean, don't get me wrong I definitely had issues; but at least I wasn't a drug addicted mother who chased after her next high, and didn't give a second thought on where food and diapers were going to come from. At least, I wasn't a loose woman who slept with any guy, who showed me just enough attention to get all my goodies. At least, I wasn't on welfare without ambitions, five kids to call my own, but by five different men. At least, I wasn't a selfish and insane mother, who decided to drive my babies into a river and watch them perish because I lost all control, mental stability, and patience. I thought since I was none of these things . . . I was entitled to have a shot at motherhood. How was it fair that God gave women like this the opportunity to mother another human being, and I could not? But, the question really was, how could I be so trivial, selfish and immature to think that way? Because even though, I lived the way I believed was right, I know that I had things in me that was wrong and definitely not suitable for raising children. I had so much pain inside my body that I oozed bitterness and spite. I was so tortured in my head from past hurt that I projected anger and rage without even meaning to. I was no better then the women who lived in a vulgar and explicit manner, because we are all sinners. Sin is not the Weight Watchers point system! In God's eyes, all sin is equal and forgivable; only humans put a point system on sin. You know what I mean, you did it before; how could tell a lie be just as wrong as killing someone in cold blood? The human mind will think that murder would definitely take the cake; but in all reality God judges all sin the same. Jesus just didn't go to the cross for one type of sin; but all sin. As I continued to let the little girl in me take control of my actions, decisions, and thoughts, I grew more and more resentful against him. I couldn't believe I was doing everything right, and still I had nothing. I had nothing but the isolation that infertility brings. I had nothing but the cold and sterile environment where doctors took my blood, examined my uterus, and put my body through countless procedures. I grew completely numb to the world around me; all I felt was my discomfort and pain. Sadness became a cancer in my body that only continued to spread. After a while, being mad illuminated my whole existence. The only conclusion that I could draw was that the Lord had abandoned my desires, and he just didn't care. At the time of my struggle, I could not understand why I had to go through such turmoil. Not being able to understand my plight made me resent and question everything. I asked myself questions like: Am I wrong for trying this hard for a baby? Am I being foolish in putting my body through yet another procedure? Maybe I'm crazy to drain my finances, time, and my emotional well being. Well, maybe God just doesn't want me to reproduce my husband's seed? I was desperate to find an answer to this pain and I resorted to frivolous thoughts, just to ease the hurt. Through this stage, I did more than try to rationalize the failure with other people flaws. My anger blamed not only my husband or the next woman who was a mother; I blamed and resented everything. I blamed my friends. I blamed my own mother. I blamed my family. I blamed God. Deep down in my own soul guilt festered and grew. I knew he didn't want to see me hurt or punish me. I hated myself for not having enough Courage to step outside of that little girl in me. I knew I had to look outside of my hurt and open my ears to hear what God was trying to tell me. But, I did not want to abandon what I wanted to accept what God wanted. I wanted my prize possession, I wanted my baby.

Looking back now, of course I feel foolish. But, it wasn't foolish at the time, not to me. I was a real human being, going through a real, real hard time. I don't want you to feel like your anger and confusion is foolish. It is very real, it is your truth and most importantly, it is a part of this journey. People, who do not know the torment of infertility, might look at us as though we are selfish. Children are not a necessity, they're a gift, and unfortunately, not all people get a chance to unwrap something so precious. We all have our desires, and even the word of God speaks on women who had these very same struggles. Wanting to be a mother is natural, and nothing new. For example, look at Hannah from the bible. Her disposition was isolated, and she wept in complete sadness because of her womb being shut off. Here is a woman who refused to eat and was taken over by complete jealousy with her husband's other wife, who had already born a number of children. She wept and prayed, wept and prayed for years without getting what she desired. I'm not saying that we as women, who desire motherhood, but haven't attained it; are justified in these emotions of being anxious, depressed, and without faith, but God knows we are human and our true feelings are not foolish. Only God sees when our hearts sink to the pit of our stomachs' every time we receive a baby shower invitation, or when we turn on our televisions, and are ambushed with yet another reality show based on pregnancy and childbirth. Only God can feel the isolation that the looks of pity on the faces of the women, who can attain pregnancy gives us. God understand that the battle with infertility can cause you to take a position of separating yourself from things that are damaging emotionally. The most important this to remember is that 99% of your energy is probably being taken up by the demands of your journey, and that is why (for myself) I had to make a conscience decision to not feel bad for my anger, frustration, and even childish actions. I could not be ashamed of letting the little girl in me to take center stage.

The point is ladies: It's okay to be sad in this journey and to resort to the little girl that lives inside of you sometimes because you are human. This journey is not for the faint at heart. At times you will feel like it has stomped it to a blood pulp and then some. It's completely typical to reach towards what you want, instead of what God is putting right in front of you. But, I had to realize, and eventually you will to realize that this journey is not entirely about your desires. I thought that my feelings were the only thing at stake, and that it was all about me. Boy was I wrong! It took me five crippling years of pain, endless fertility procedures, destructive behavior, and sleepless nights to realize that God was not abandoning my goal. And, even though I never quite got the answer for knowing why I had to go through so much pain, but I did have a revelation. And, even though I want to be sensitive to the women who are having this struggle . . . I owe it to you to be entirely truthful. Your questions may never be answered, the way you want or expect. The truth is that you may very well come out this thing without what you expected and wanted the most. But one thing is for certain, this journey will come to an end. Either way it ends, I promise you that it will end to start a brand new journey, birthing new life and new possibilities. This journey will serve not as your failure, but your testimony to help others.

The reason that I put Deuteronomy 32:4 in the very beginning of this chapter is because, even though my questioning to God for my pain wasn't answered to my liking; I have indeed gained an understanding that the Lord is perfect in all his ways. I know that you can't see past your pain in the present moment, but time will reveal to you the same truth. Even if we feel like it's unfair and cruel, his way is always the way. See, God operates in truth, love, commandments and not emotions. Yes, he loves us to no end; but he left us with instructions in how to live, and coexist with our brother. He didn't tell us to wing it, or deal with people based on our emotions towards them. See, the conflict with this is as women, we feel things with our hearts and not with our minds, making our own rules. Making our decisions with our heart and emotions then allows us to live without standards, boundaries, and rules, and it only ends with a potential recipe for disaster.

You know I'm telling the truth! We will stay with men who take from us physically, emotional, and mentally because our hearts LOVE them. We forget about our own well beings, just to say we have love from a man. We allow a man to fill the emptiness of our beds when we are really trying to fulfill the emptiness in our souls. If God wanted us to live without rules and standards, we wouldn't have word. Let's be honest, the experience of infertility (or going through any struggle) is nothing but heart strings, and vulnerability and we can't see past wanting that baby, instead of seeking what he requires from and for us. We become blind by our motivation to fulfill our dreams, whether it is a baby, wedding, or career. We forget to seek God's plan for our lives, and I believe we make our mistakes there because we don't trust God enough to wait for his answers or plans for us. We get in the way, and try our best to make things happen on our own and that's why we make messes out of our lives. We wonder why it is that a husband won't do right, and it's all because God may not have intended for that man to be your husband. We wonder why our career choice is not coinciding with our happiness, maybe it's because that is not the path God is directing you to follow. One of the most profound, yet simple things that I have learned through this journey is to trust God and his plans for me. I know that me telling you that God works being perfect doesn't tell you what you want to know. I know you want to know when you will meet your desired baby or the breakthrough in your specific situation, but I truly believe that God allows us to go through specific struggles for a reason that we don't understand until it's over. I know it sounds cliché, and one of the worse parts of this journey for me was listening to the much unneeded advice and "clichés". My all time LEAST favorites while going through my journey were: "Gods does everything for a reason", and "It's just not your time yet". I would become livid because the people that would give me advice would be women who'd never had to struggle to have a baby. I mean, it seemed like their husbands would only have to stare at them too hard, and BAM! They would pop up pregnant! How could you know how this feels, when you've never experience such grief? When you have walked in the shoes of a infertile woman; waking up every morning to give yourself a needle of hormone injections; injecting four inch needles into your buttocks filled with more hormones, going to the doctor's office everyday for weeks at a time; putting your feet on stirrups on a daily basis, and feeling like your are being violated with a clamp, because the doctors' insensitively shoves it in your vagina, repeatedly taking phone calls from a nurse who tells you that your pregnancy test was negative with an uncompassionate tone, like you didn't just go through a month long process, or crying everyday because you're physically, and emotionally tired of everything . . . Then, maybe the "average fertile woman", who only had to lie or her back to conceive, could actually understand the day to day struggle of the "infertile woman" to get pregnant. When you are going through this journey, the clichés can literally kill some part of you, making you feel as if no one understands, and that you are all alone in your endeavors. So, please don't take the cliché of not understanding your plight with infertility until it's over in a negative manner. It is close to impossible to comprehend anything while you are experiencing debilitating pain at the hands of your tussle with infertility; or any struggle that you may face. It wasn't until my journey with infertility was over that I gained a complete understanding of God's mercy. Through the process of my journey, I realized how much of a mess I really was. By the end of it, I was so relieved that after all my mistakes and tantrums; God stilled loved me and accepted me despite me allowing childlike tactics to destroy the relationship I had with him. He chooses to still want me and that is nothing short of amazing. I realized that my blessing is not of my own merit, because I deserve nothing. I finally could allow the little girl in me to fade in the background. God was gracious enough to give me what I needed, even though I worked hard to sabotage my life with my anger, and that anger is what takes us to the next part of this journey.

Chapter Two

Using Destruction for a Band Aid

Still Raining

Job 36:27; "For he maketh small the drops of water: they pour down rain according to the vapor thereof"

It's beginning to rain again
Why is it raining now?
It rained yesterday
And the forecast predicts it'll rain tomorrow
I can still smell the dew, but it's not sweet
The rain has softened the earth around me and now
mud
covers my feet
I can't even speak
I'm silenced by the downpour
Life is drowsy and everything is moving in slow motion
My pain defeats me
And leaves me
Miserably
Alone
The enemy got me thinking that no one cares
But maybe that's the truth because no one is here
I began to think that even Jesus turned a deaf ear
To the whining in my voice
Or the stupidity of my choice
In losing faith in him
But the walls are closing in
They are just inches from my skin
Then the sun peaks in

I begin to feel the warmth upon my face
It's getting warmer and I know this feeling, I'm familiar
with his amazing grace
I said I know this feeling; I'm familiar with his amazing
grace
I feel the angels setting up camp around me
Their arms are consoling me
He's beginning to breathe life back into me
Reminding me of the promises he has given me
And to never let the adversary steal them
Even if for now, I can't believe them
The rain has stopped again
It's not raining now
But will it rain tomorrow
Because today, these tears are not falling

(Proverbs 17:19) "He who loves a quarrel loves sin, he who builds a high gate invites destruction" KJV

(Proverbs 2:12-14) "Wisdom will save you from the ways of wicked men, from men whose words are perverse, who leaves the straight paths to walk in dark ways, who delight in doing wrong and rejoice in the perverseness of evil" KJV

*I*n this part of my journey, I willingly became acquainted with destruction. Contrary to the beginning leg of this journey, my pain encompassed more anger than childlike sadness and expectations. By, this time of the journey, we had experienced a chemical pregnancy; which is when the egg is fertilized, but it does not implant in the uterus and it basically frizzles away. We also had experienced two early miscarriages, in which the doctor only explained as a chromosome abnormality. He explained it was common and it only meant that the embryo was not strong enough to flourish in the womb. Here we were; finally relieved and excited about getting our baby; just for our dreams to be snatched away so harshly and quickly. All I was left with was a broken heart; severe cramps, and bleeding profusely.

I just refused to keep coping with my loss; the miscarriages' were lethal, but the unanswered questions were harsher. No one could offer up answers. Not the doctors, preacher man, or God. I just wanted to know why this kept happening to me, it took me so long to finally get pregnant, and then the pregnancies were taken from me. Every fiber of my being was on fire, all I can see was red, and before long, I wanted someone or something to pay for my pain. The inner child in me was becoming this demonic force that enclosed pain and havoc. I begin to think that I was justified to do anything because I already was paying the price of being miserable. I was so angry, and desperate. I was so desperate for anyone to tell me anything or give me a glimpse of hope; I started to internalize and take everything to heart. What I mean is that, if I was watching the Christian network and a prophet gave a prophetic word; I assumed they were talking directly to me because I wanted someone to talk to me. I wanted someone to tell me that the suffering was about to come to an abrupt and welcomed end. I wanted to believe that this journey was finally coming to a stop, and I could be happy with my little baby, with the sweetest aroma and baby breath. I wanted someone to tell me exactly when the pain was going to stop, or even pause for a moment. I wanted my baby, and that was all I could see. Before long, I found myself in desperate need of any type of comfort. By now, we'd been through Clomid therapy, IUIs, and even IVF. In Vitro Fertilization is definitely the most abrasive, expensive, and time consuming fertility option. What happens is that the doctors stimulate a woman's eggs through medication after a small period of shutting the woman's system down. This small period is used to quiet the woman's reproduction organs to get ready for the stimulation. The woman then, inject three to four medications into her abdomen to jump start egg production and this is closely monitored with daily doctor visits. Once the eggs are mature and ready to ovulate; the women has a small, surgical procedure, where the doctors retrieve the eggs. Once the eggs are taken, the eggs are combined with her spouse's sperm in a dish. If all goes well, the eggs are fertilized and put back into the women in a 3-5 day span. The woman has to wait two weeks to see if the embryos had attached and growing normally. Although, I just gave you a brief overall of what the procedure consist of; no one can prepare you for the dedication and strong will that must be apart of your approach to just get through the procedure. No one can prepare you on going through such a precise regimen and emotional roller coaster, just to fail and still be without your baby. I would start the cycle with excitement, joy, and hope. By time I entered into mid cycle, I would grow tired and weary with the daily visits and tight medication schedule. Then, towards the end you become nervous and anxious with the egg quality, because if you had a bad stimulation response; chances that your egg quality is not even sufficient to with stand the actually In Vitro Fertilization procedure. Then, if all goes well with your embryos and they are good enough for the transfer; I would become elated because in my head, I was pregnant. Then the emotional roller coaster takes a huge dip when the pregnancy test says . . . . Negative. Then, the sadness turns into determination to get ready to enter the next cycle. But, nothing prepared me or my marriage for the devastation.

My marriage was my first target for destruction to prevail. You would think that my husband and I had this thing to a science; that this would have forced us closer together. Instead we started to grow apart, and the tragedies were pushing a thicker wedge between us. We'd both allowed our frustration with infertility and failed pregnancies to make us independent of each other. I can't think of anything worse than independence to destroy a union that is based on unity and cohabitation. When a union is based on unity and cohabitation, independence can become lethal, and single handedly destroy something that was once so beautiful. Sabotaging my marriage, at this time, became my blissful entertainment, because everything else around me was a sorrowful tragedy.

This period of the journey was my darkest hour, and I'd convinced myself that I needed to find comfort, outside of my marriage. Whether it was food, drugs, self inflicting pain, or other people . . . I was on a mission to find some type of pain reliever, because Tylenol just wasn't cutting it! I found that my husband no longer filled that emptiness that I felt. I'm reminded of a time during this journey when my husband and I made love. It was a rare occasion that we even had sexual relations during this point of the journey, because of our disdain for one another, and the whole process of infertility. I remember so vividly during the height of our sexual encounter, demanding my husband to thrust deeper in me; harder. But, it was a frantic demand, and not a steamy one. The urgency for his thrust was as though he was thrusting something vital inside of me; like filling me back up with the happiness and passion for life that infertility was draining from me. My mind convinced me that he could forcefully push something inside of me that could fill the emptiness that was in me. Looking back, I knew in my heart that nothing could heal the isolation, and emptiness that I felt. Sex just wasn't the key.

The adversity really played on my vulnerability and anger, because at the time I was convinced that my husband stopped caring about me and our situation. I can recall my husband's behavior towards me during our entire second IVF attempt. I remember feeling so alone in that whole cycle, because my husband was disconnected throughout the ordeal. Unlike, my first IVF, my parents was aware of the situation, and on board. So, after my egg retrieval, my husband and parents drove me home. Like a real mother, my mom got me situated, set me up on the couch because she had to leave for work, and didn't want me climbing the stairs. She offered me words of support, all while she prepared my lunch. My husband was nowhere to be found; he disappeared as soon as he saw my parents catering to my every need. What he didn't know was; even though the gentle stroke of my mothers hands, and security of my father's presence, served as my saving grace . . . I wanted those hands and secure presence to belong to my husband. At the end of the day, I was putting my body through so many traumas for him and me to become parents, for him to become the father that he so desperately wanted to be. It was a decision that we'd made together, yet he was not there by my side when I needed him the most and I felt alone. Before long, my parents had to leave, but before my mom left, she called my husband down and told him to look after me. My thoughts were consumed with making reasons to excuse his poor and insensitive behavior. I could not understand why my mother had to tell him to look after his own wife; who just recently underwent surgery at his expense. I was putting my body through stress, just to give him a child and someone other them himself had to remind him to be there for me. I was in too much pain to argue, and even more embarrassed in front of my parents. After my parents left, I remember asking him to get me a drink of water. He obliged, and then went back upstairs;

leaving me totally alone. Tears started to burn my eyes and I violently pushed them away because I was so tired of being hurt by his insensitivity. I could not comprehend why he was acting so trivial by ignoring my need for his attention. I know that he could not take the physically pain away from the egg retrieval; but he could of soothe the emotional strain with his kind words and desire to want to comfort me. Nevertheless, I trooped on alone, taking my pain meds just to get some sleep.

After awakening, I had to go to the bathroom, and my yells for assistance were too low for my husband to hear. The pain had intensified to such a degree that I couldn't bring my voice loud enough to call to him any longer, so eventually I crawled on my hands and knees until I got myself to the toilet. By this time I was finally close enough to the steps to call again, but didn't. The sounds of his Xbox filled my ears, and all I could do was cry. I just couldn't understand why he wasn't down stairs helping his wife. I was in need of his help and compassion! He should have been rubbing my face, and kissing my cheeks. He should have been cuddled up on the couch with me, asking if I needed anything. Instead, he was playing his Xbox, while I pulled myself onto the toilet. In that incident, something died. I no longer felt obligated to care about anyone else's feelings or needs, which didn't care about mine. In that moment I felt justified for the things that I had in mind to do. I felt so alone, and the person, who was supposed to have my back, did not. My husband was supposed to be my outlet, my comfort zone, but he was becoming what everyone else was to be . . . a distant memory.

I often wondered why all of sudden, the communication and bond between us stopped. First, I solely blamed myself because I was increasingly becoming someone that we both disliked. I would nag and cry all the time because of the strain of the treatments, and failed pregnancies. Another reason why I had to own some fault in the breakdown of our relationship was because something that I allowed to take root early on in our courtship had proven to destroy our present and future. In the beginning of my relationship with my husband, I was so head strong and determined that I did not need a man for anything. I was an independent woman and no man needed to be accountable for me. I made my own decisions and I didn't need or desired any help. A man was designed to lead, provide, and protect; but I didn't need any part of that truth. I never gave my husband the chance to be my leader; the person that I needed. I made life so easy for him, taking most of the responsibility for everything from finances, to the day to day hustle and bustle. I was raised to be a powerhouse and strong willed individual; what need did I have for authority? Why should he feel the need to cater to me when I'd allowed him to think about himself solely throughout our relationship thus far, or gave the impression that I was too strong to need anyone or anything? Who was I to finally demand that respect or wish, to finally put him in the position to be the man God designed all males to be? Even though I knew all the things that I just mentioned to be true, I somehow thought that since he wasn't required to be there for me any other time, this would be the time that he would step up and want to. How could he lie in bed beside me, hear my painful cries, and not put his arms around me? How could he say he loved me, but didn't want to do anything to make me happy in such a miserable time? Why didn't he have enough common sense to take every chance he got to love on me, write me a love letter; put a silly note in my lunch bag; buy me flowers; or just acknowledge my pain? How could he continually watch me walk through hell in gasoline underwear, for the sake of his legacy, and not be compelled to comfort me?

Ladies, I know on this very difficult road, being cradled and loved is necessary. It's no way that you can do this without that support. You need someone to hold your hand and keep you on your feet, sometimes literally. There were times when I fell to the floor, on my knees in complete despair, because I just couldn't take it anymore, and then I got up, looked around and I was by myself. That's why it was so important for me to write this love letter to women, who are going through an ordeal similar to my own, especially if they are without love and support. You need someone to stay consistent in caring about you, and what you are going through, in spite of their personal feelings and opinions.

My marriage was continuing to crumble. We grew silent towards one another, and had nothing to say. My husband shut me out, and I reciprocated his attitude to the point where our disdain for each other and our situation put an end to our intimacy between one another. I believe, after awhile, it was just too hard for either of us to deal with the disappointment, and grief. It was overwhelming to the point of our relationship falling apart in chunks around us, and there was just no energy left to care enough to fix it. Over time, my resentment festered and grew into something ugly, something that I didn't recognize within myself. The man that I'd loved since my teenage years was becoming someone that disgusted me. We'd lost so much time and faith, neither of us was trying to do anything to heal it. We just refused to deal with it. My husband ignored my plea for comfort and intimacy; when I did ask, and I knew it was my anger that forced him away. Even when he tried, I would become hesitant and unsure. The same fingertips that I longed for suddenly made my skin crawl. His anger and resentment started to match mine, and because of his inability to communicate his anger; it just grew and grew silently. One thing, I can admit is that during this stage, it was all about my feelings, I'd put it in my mind that since my husband didn't have to physically endure this struggle, like I did, he wasn't being affected like I was. Since, he couldn't articulate his feelings or even use gestures . . . I believed he just didn't care. So, eventually all of this ugliness convinced me that we were done, and divorce was in our immediate future. I was convinced that I could find a better man; one who would love and appreciate me. My marriage was holding on by a thread, and I was ready to snap or yank it loose, not because we didn't love one another, but because we didn't know how to communicate and grieve with each other. We were doing it separately, causing more destruction. The fights got more intense, and we let resentment speak for us in our arguments. I am reminded of a time when I was so upset at him that I cut him so deeply with my words. I told him that it was probably God not wanting us to get pregnant because he wasn't man enough to be a husband, more less a father. I remember the chilly look on his face after I said it, and I also remember feeling like dirt, yet it gave me a feeling of empowerment. I wanted to hurt him so bad because he was hurting me. He was killing me with his silence and dislike for me. Have you ever been in a marriage or relationship where you felt that the person you were with, hated you, and looked to everyone but you for comfort? Well, if you have, then you can understand my need for revenge. I wanted to hurt him because I was hurt with his actions and attitude towards me.

All of this nonsense in my marriage was destruction, and I used it as my band aid. It actually just covered up the scar so it wouldn't look so ugly. I used it to cover up the pain that I was feeling, so that people couldn't see it. I can recall times when people who ask my husband and I, "You guys been together for eternity, when are y'all going to pop out some babies?" Only if they knew the pain that we'd endured because of our inability to do so. But, instead of us expressing the truth, and feelings on the matter, we would come up with excuses that I was waiting to finish college or that we were just enjoying the honeymoon stage of our marriage. It was all lies, and we found ourselves being strained by infertility, and pretending that it did not exist. It was important that we showed the world that we were okay, even if it was a lie. Even though we were killing each other emotionally behind closed doors, I still wanted everyone to think that I was happy; that we were happy. So, because we couldn't articulate our pain to the world, we did it through destroying one another's pride and self esteem. It was easier for me to deal with things in a destructive manner, because it served as an outlet to my anger. Don't look surprised, isn't it easier to do the things we are not supposed to do, versus working harder to do what is right? Sin feels good. How many of us have fallen in the traps of fornication? We fall because it's inviting, and it feels good. It satisfies our itch for a little while. So, if you find yourself in this part of the journey, it's normal, because you feel that desperate to be comforted at any cost.

See, destruction makes us blind to the mess that we are actually making of the situation. It only serves as a distraction, and it's only temporary, because at the end of the day, I still found myself at sadness's door. See, separating ourselves from God through sin, only intensified and worsened our situations, it literally killed us spiritually, emotionally, and mentally. But, that truth didn't stop my behavior, I continued to choose destruction to comfort me, and validate my thoughtless actions. It only masked the hurt that I was feeling inside, because I couldn't confront it yet. So, I just continued to act out. My marriage wasn't the only thing I allowed destruction to have for a moment. I gave it my self esteem and self worth. Growing up, my mother; and everyone around me, has always made me painfully aware that I was a bigger girl than the average female, and it seemed as if she worked overtime to keep me from the fate of obesity. She was somewhat extreme about it. I remember being eight years old and wearing a girdle. I can remember one specific day when I first started to wear a girdle. I was forced to tears because the elastic stuck into my skin so deeply that it began to burn, making it painful just to walk. That situation taught me that I had to do anything to hide who I really was and that I should be so ashamed of my body that I would do anything to change it. So, things only intensified; I was introduced to diet pills by eighteen, and obsessed with fad diets. Although being told that I was just too big, and my mother's extreme measures taking a toll on my self esteem, I do believe she was coming from a good and concerned place. She wanted to save me from the diseases that plagued our family, like: diabetes and hypertension. Despite her good intentions, her methods were wrong.

Weight has always been a constant struggle for me, and also the source of me being teased and tormented throughout my life. At this specific time of infertility, that insecurity was heightened to the tenth power. I remember being completely devastated when my mother reasoned that I wasn't getting pregnant because I was too fat. I don't believe she had malicious intentions when she said those hurtful words, because she's always been a very blunt and outspoken individual. So, at the time; I was just too fragile and overwhelmed with the things that were going on in my life to be able to handle a blow so hard. That on top of the fact that she'd taunted me with comments like this my entire life, I never got use to it, and it never stop hurting. I learned to grow a thick skin early on, and that is what allowed me to own the capability of masking my feelings and putting on a tough front. With infertility in my life, that tough skin was useless. I was glass and everything threatened to break me. I took her words and internalized each and every syllable, convincing myself that I *was* too fat to get pregnant! Hey, at least now in my own head, I could now justify my battle with infertility. I thought that I'd finally found my answer. If I lost a large amount of weight, it would be the trick. I was desperate, and this seemed to be the key, so I resorted to throwing up my food. Yes, at first it was to serve as weight management, but it turned into a relief from this infertility roller coaster, and all the feelings I harbored from being told I was fat, huge, and big boned my entire life. Literally, as my finger was releasing recently digested food, I felt liberated. It freed me from not being good enough for my mother, the kids who teased me when I was younger, and the baby that I was so desperate to have. I was letting go of something that was burdening me, the problem was; it wasn't food. I wanted to release the pain and confusion in regards to why I wasn't getting pregnant, or why I couldn't hold my pregnancies. For those few moments, throwing up the food I consumed gave me a sense of accomplishment. I didn't have to fight for what I wanted, like I had to do through the infertility treatments. Throwing up my food also made me feel like I had control and power over something; anything. In my head, I was taking charge and helping myself get to my ultimate goal. I convinced myself that I would not let fat, get in the way of achieving my dreams of being a mother. I also convinced myself that this would change my feelings towards myself of feeling inferior to self esteem, self worth, and my body image.

This leg of my walk through this journey, I sank lower in my darkness and despair. I completely lost myself in the pain and struggle. I allowed my anger to turn me into a person, which I did not recognize and was ashamed of. At this point I dwindled down to nothing; zero. In my eyes everyone was my enemy and I had no God, husband, friends, family, dreams, or a will to live. I had allowed my anger towards myself and my situation to create such a mess and to shut my heart off to everyone and everything around me. But, in spite of my anger towards everyone, I still prayed that someone would love me enough to recognize my demise and save me. I just wanted someone to look past my exterior and recognize my screams for help. Yes, at this point, my cries had turned to a full blown screams, but no one came, no one would serve as my hero; no one could be my salvation. I wanted someone to touch all the hurting spots within me, and no one had the power to do that. And even though I knew it was physically impossible for a person to do that, I at least wanted someone to just massage and caress the spots; in my mind that would have lessened my pain. It seemed like the closest people to me didn't even try to understand my anger; they felt that my efforts in pursuing motherhood was too physically, emotionally, and mentally taxing to my well being. Their wish and advice was just to cease and release my dreams of becoming a mother. They owned a mentally that if it was meant to be, then it would naturally happen; seeking artificial methods was not the solution. For me, I compared it to someone telling a cancer patient not to take chemotherapy, and then telling them, "If it's meant for you to live, then you will". That is crazy, who would not want to live? Who would reject medical treatment and interventions to better the quality of their own lives? Even though infertility is not physically life threatening; it does kill a part of your soul, and it makes you fight for your right to live the way you desire.

Self destruction could no longer be my band aid; it was supposed to hide the scar until it healed, and it was not doing its job anymore. The band aid that was supposed to be assisting in helping me was only assisting in killing me. Harboring this pain was crippling and I did it only because I didn't want the world to know I was a real human being, going through real pain. I didn't want to be embarrassed and judged by people in their limited intellectual capabilities in understanding just what infertility means and how devastated the process could be. The people that I had personal relationships with were judgmental, so how could I expect empathy or anything more from the world. I can recall a time when a relative told me that infertility treatments were useless, because it was artificial, and not the way God intended for children to be conceived. Their theory was: if God didn't do it the natural way, it was not meant to be. So, why keep putting myself through the agony of infertility procedures, if it is not meant to be? Their statements did more than kill my hope. They placed judgment on my personal decision, which was more than brutal to my feelings. The whole point of judgment is experience. Doesn't a judge (or someone that is judging a situation) use their knowledge and experience, in the given matter, to assess the situation and make a sound conclusion? So, if they did not experience infertility, then how could they judge me and my decision to pursue my goals in having a child? And, even if my relative couldn't agree with my decision; they could have just been supportive and sensitive to my ordeal.

It was time for me to be healed from all the drama, non-supportive love ones, my past, and the stupid notion that the destruction that I allowed to become me was actually healing me. I thought that destruction would be my source of healing or my "bit of relief"; but it was only me retaliating against God, and everyone who I felt left me alone and stranded in this strife alone. I wanted to punish God for his refusal to change my situation on my terms, I wanted the infertility to be over so, I thought I could hurt God with my disobedience. In hindsight, I realized that I was already dead. I had turned my back on Christ, and turned to sin and destruction, which represented death in its ugliest form. And, being dead, at this specific time, wasn't so bad because I hated everything about my situation. I hated everything about myself, and to die would have meant relief from the torture of this life. It seemed that everything that I struggled with, before my infertility journey, started to surface more and more each day, because I was in such a dark place. Things that happened to me in elementary school came up. It took me to the exact same place that had left me feeling like I could trust no one. It took me to a place that I thought I'd left behind . . . a place I thought I'd cleaned the blood up from the wound, and should now only be dealing with the scar. But, the wounds were still open, and the biggest one was on its way to bleed to death and a bandage could not contain it.

The wound that was just becoming to big to contain, was being sexually abused and molested by female relatives. It took me back to the floor where I would just lay paralyzed and wonder, why is this happening, or how could they choose me? I trusted these people, even looked up to them, they made me feel so secure with them. My abusers were not strangers; they were family that I enjoyed spending time with and they used my admiration for them to their advantage. Although, the experience was very traumatic and confusing at first; by long my love for them allowed me to accept the pleasure from the abuse and to protect their actions.

One memory that I can recall and sticks in my head like gum to the ground, and above all my experiences with the sexual abuse; was the first time it happened. I was in a slumber party with my about four of my female relatives; something that was not uncommon. I love the slumber parties because we were allowed to eat all the pizza and candy that our bodies could digest. I especially loved being the youngest because it was such a treat for me to listen to the wild stories that my older relatives had about school, money, and boys. I loved being made to feel like I was on their level and they made it a point to always fill me in on what to do or not to do with the boys. I felt like I had the advantage on all my peers because I had a front row seat in teen life; while they were still stuck at ten! This specific sleepover wasn't much different than the previous; I burnt out first and settled in my sleeping bag while the others were still enjoying themselves. My next memory was being woken up to my molester suckling my breast, and the other pinning me down. I remember being so confused and flinching at the pain of the forceful sucking. I remember clinching my eyes so tight . . . afraid of letting the tears escape. I just wanted it to be over and run away. I wanted to run from the shame and embarrassment, so I did; but only in my mind. The toughing and groping went on for what felt like an eternity. I believe my flinching from the pain was a clear indictor that I was uncomfortable because by long she slowed up and began to be very gentle and soothing. I recall her voice being so soft and seductive. She kept telling me that she was just trying to make me feel good and if I loved them; I would make them feel the same way.

I could not escape the abuse that night; but I did find an escape. Allowing myself to run away to false security is only a representation of the next wound. I found a way to run away from the pain; I used inhalants to help me escape the shame and embarrassment. It didn't solve my issues, but it served as a relief from my pain, even if it was only for a few moments. I remember running to the bathroom and locking the door. I would reach for the linen closet and pull out my old, dusty Reebok tennis shoe, and a can of oil sheen that I had masterfully hidden. My heart would race in excitement and anticipation, because I knew that I was about to blackout and escape everything that hurt me. My molesters, the kids that served as monsters; who would tease me mercilessly, the feeling of not being desirable or good enough for anyone, and the desperate need I had for love and acceptance. I would put the tennis shoe over my mouth and nose and cock the shoe to the side, so that I could put the nozzle in it. Then I would spray until I was not coherent and totally blacked out. When I woke up, my problems were still there and I was still hurt; but those moments were precious because I didn't have to think about the shame and embarrassment that defined my life. I didn't have to deal with not being good enough for my mother, who expected me to be the expression of perfection. I didn't have to worry about being the preacher's kid, who people put on a pedestal and expected to talk, walk, and act as holy as the angels. I didn't have to deal with not being good enough for the bullies who cut me down every day with their words on my physical appearance and my shortcomings of my nose being too wide, skin being too dark; and my feet being too long. I didn't have to be reduced to someone's deranged sexual expectation. It was just me and the quiet.

With the pain of my failed attempts at pregnancy, and my past baggage, I knew I was damaged goods. The pain of molestation left me hurt and confused. For a long time I believed that I was supposed to be a lesbian. How else could I rationalize the fact that my abusers were females? Maybe I gave some type of lesbian vibes bouncing off of me, that made these females choose me; I had no idea what is was. I was just a child trying to make sense of, and justify the chaos. Molestation gave me a distorted way of thinking about sex, and those thoughts followed me throughout my adolescent and teenage years. It made me afraid of two things: pursuing normal, healthy relationships with men and relationships with people in general. First it was: Am I pretty enough or desirable enough for a man? I really believed in my heart that I only appealed to women because of my previous experiences and again how my abusers were females. Secondly, I didn't feel good enough to be loved by anyone. I was constantly being told how big I was or how dark I was, and that allowed me to believe that no one could ever accept me for who I was. Even when I found love with a man . . . I still struggled with accepting it because I didn't truly believe that someone could actually want me. I didn't feel like I was fit to be someone's true source of affection. I felt like I was only capable of being their sexual exploration. That's what sexual abuse did to me. It left me feeling like I was someone's distorted sexual secret, and they could do whatever they wanted with me. I felt that sex or things of a sexual nature were dirty, grimy, and should remain secretive. Sexual abuse taught me how to use my body for the acceptance and affection I really wanted, and it taught me to give into one's desire, so that I would feel wanted and appreciated. When someone is exposed to sexual conduct, at a tender and impressionable age, they tend to confuse it with love instead of the filth that it really is. I was no exception. Sexual abuse, substance abuse, bullying, unrealistic expectations from my mother; the people pleasing mentality, and the infertility I had was taking an absolute toll on my well being. I knew I needed help, and a breakthrough. This was the time in my journey where I realized that I had to find true healing before I could think about molding another human being and becoming a mother. Coming to this realization was vital to my breakthrough, but it didn't come without anger. I knew that giving up on pursing motherhood at that time was necessary because I had a lot of work to do for my own personal survival and growth. Even though relief came with this, anger did too because the last thing I wanted to do was abandon the biggest dream I'd ever had. Ever since I was eighteen, I had the same dream often. I dreamt that I was holding a little girl with a light complexion and a bushy ponytail. My heart knew that it was only a matter of time before I met her, I didn't care what my family, friends, mentors, or even doctors said. Everyone told me to just give up. My doctors even told me that there is nothing else they could do for me. But, my heart couldn't let go of that little girl that I clutched on to for dear life; the little girl that was literally of my dreams. But, I knew that our meeting had to be delayed because I was in a place where life just did not exist. I eventually packed away all the baby magazines and prenatal DVDs. I couldn't stand to see pregnant women, go to baby showers; or even watch a program on television where babies were the focus. When shows like: Babies Stories, Adoption Stories, Runway Mom, and Deliver Me decorated the time slots, it was all I could do to stay away! I even packed away my hope chest, the same hope chest I started shortly after I dreamt about that little girl. It was a tote that I purchased from Wal-Mart, and I'd filled it with baby items that I would buy from work. Of course, I worked at a Babies R Us; I wanted to be in a place where I could see the realization of everything that I hoped for. I could see the round and protruding bellies wobbling around the store. I would see brand new babies being cradled by their mothers and I wanted nothing more to be able to first handedly live that reality.

It was time for me to put my dream on the back burner, and concentrate on putting myself back together again. The distance that I walked thus far on the journey had me feeling completely done; helpless. I was ready for a breakthrough, a new beginning. I was ready to welcome a renewed spirit and restoration of health and happiness. I was ready to expose all of my wounds, so the band aids had to come off, so they could properly heal.

Chapter 3

Words to Live By

Replenish

I need you to greet me with a kiss every morning that I rise
Because yesterday took everything I had
The affection of your kiss fills me back up
And inspires me to use my feet to stomp through the
wilderness
I need you to hug me as soon as my eyes open to the
dawn
Its supplies my spirit with the encouragement that life
demolished yesterday
Make me whole again with the softness of your touch
Let it nourish the empty that sits at the pit of my
stomach
Because yesterday ate up my determination to just
breathe
Replenish me
Replenish me
So, that I may be whole again
So that I may live inside the noise of the world again
So that I might appreciate the simplicity of the air again

(Luke 15; 18; 19; 24) "I will arise and go to my father, and I will say to him, "Father, I have sinned against heaven and before you. I am no longer worthy to be called your son. For this my son was dead, and is alive again; he was lost, and is found".

*J*could not have picked a better scripture to outline my transition to this leg of the journey. Words cannot describe how much the distance thus far had changed me. Even though, a lot of negative came out of it, positivity still loomed around me and I needed every drop of it. I felt that I was beginning to be replenished with life again and had accepted the realization of a change. I was ready to take on life again, and I finally was beginning to look at myself for who I was, and that was one of the scariest things I ever had to do. I had to look at all my flaws and imperfections when I already felt so low; but it was vital for me to see and accept my truth, that I may continue successfully towards the finish line. I had to make a conscious decision to do the hard work, and to work through the things that had gotten me to that dead place. I did not want to be blind to the factualness of who I have become any longer. I did not want to use destruction and false methods to ease the pain anymore. I was ready to courageously face my problems, work through them, and release any memory of them; so that I could really live and redefine who I was. I had to give up the control that I actually never had to begin with. I once thought that I could control everything including my quest to get pregnant; I was sadly mistaken. I was now realizing that control aspect in me had to die. The manipulating nature that I used to get my way had to cease. It was time to redefine who

I was, by making changes in my habits and personality. That's why the story of the prodigal son hit home for me; it pulled right on my heartstrings. I felt like I was coming back to God, and acknowledging that he was in complete control of my destiny; even if I did not agree with the direction he was taking me to get there. I was finding myself back in the safe arms of Christ from the darkest, dirtiest hole. I no longer felt comforted by the lust and pleasure of sin. I no longer felt that I was justified to sin and to intentionally disrespect God because I was hurting. I no longer thought that I should retaliate against God, because I couldn't figure out why I kept doing the right things without making progress or attaining the success that I desired. I was ready to reverse my path on this journey and the direction that I was headed. It was time to walk straight.

At this time of my journey, my husband and I were not going through any infertility treatments. We both accepted it was time to step back and heal our individual selves, and our marriage. I personally accepted that I was a chaotic mess; a ball of utter confusion! I knew that I had no business trying to mother another human being when I needed to be mothered and nurtured. At this time, nurture played a vital part of my recovery. By this time, I was on miscarriage number three and totally burnt out. Even though this was definitely the turning point of my journey, I was at my emotional lowest. I was totally dimmed at this point. The light that once filled my eyes was gone. Almost all hope was gone; my mind swirled constantly around the emptiness and pain that the miscarriages and failure provided. My eyes were a blank stare, and I didn't recognize myself when I looked in the mirror. It was as if I were only the shell of what I once was. I was definitely at the point where I couldn't take anymore. I was tired of my own foolishness. I was tired of all the people that I allowed to surround me because they were similar to me. They allowed darkness to rule their worlds because of the dissatisfactions of life. But, the difference between us now, was that I was ready to change.

Even though my new revelation of getting myself back to a healthy and safe place was in full gear, I begun to move into what I called the guilty snippet of the journey. My conscience was getting the best of me at this time, because I felt so guilty for allowing myself to turn away from God's arms. The same God that has been my refuge so many times before, I didn't trust enough to get me through this infertility experience along with my other problems. I fought tooth and nail against myself during this time because I just couldn't believe that I allowed myself to become the very person that my mother had raise me not to be; an intentional sinner. My guilt for becoming that, made me feel like a waste of space. I eventually got through this rough patch with lots of prayer and nurturing people. This part of the journey, I needed a soft and nurturing approach because I was so broken. So, when I did build a little confidence, I needed to protect that, because I wasn't stable enough to take criticism yet. I was still very much affected by what people thought or said about me at this point of my recovery. In hindsight, I had to go through this stage alone and without a selected few. I actually had to be without some friends and family because of my sensitivity at this very critical turning point in this journey. I had to protect myself from things and persons, who had the ability to hurt me with their very blunt, opinionated, judgmental views on the things that were going on in my life. The very least bit of criticism would have set me back. I can recollect the time, where I had to make the definite decision to exclude people from this leg in the journey.

One day after a long day of work, and at an end of an unsuccessful invitro fertilization procedure; my mother asked for me to meet her at her home; alone. My initial reaction was to deny her invitation because for her to ask me to come without my husband, was a red flag. And, even though I knew my mother had the capabilities to break my spirits with her bullheaded and uncompromising demeanor, part of me was busy hoping for a compassionate side. For the life of me, I wanted her to handle me with a soft poise, because I needed my mother, not a dictator or a judge. I needed her to hold my hand and tell me that I had her support through all of this. I needed her shoulder to cry on. I needed her ears to listen to my venting, for me to tell her just how unfair it was for me to go through all of this to have a baby. Instead, I was bombarded with slurs that accused me of not being mentally well. She suggested that I needed to go see a shrink because I was on the verge of a mental breakdown. I can not put in words how hurtful this encounter with my mother was, it was so painful that I got up and walked out half way through the ordeal. My mother and I didn't speak for months, but that didn't stop my quest for a complete healing.

Well, my recovery was fast approaching, and once God spoke, it didn't take long before the healing was being manifested. It must have been destined! I say that because things just fell in place. Two months had past and some powerful things were happening. God resurrected some healthy relationships in my life, my marriage seemed to have turned all the way around, I had this new drive and confidence to want to reach out to people for help. The new drive that I had, to finally reach out for help, was about to be tested because contrary to my better judgment; I decided to go ahead and do another IVF. I knew it was too soon, but because I was feeling so renewed because of all the positivity that was going on. I had my energy back and a new pep in my step. I felt ready to restart this journey and I wanted with every part of me to believe that it was time to continue on towards the finish line to end this journey of infertility.

The cycle went fast and I found myself at the end of my in vitro fertilization cycle and I was at work when I received a call from my nurse from the fertility center. I was waiting for the results of the blood test that determined the future of my unborn baby. You would think that news of a positive pregnancy test was the most gratifying news that an expecting "hopeful" mother would want; but this case was different. See, my hormones levels were dangerously low for my gestational age and it was a good chance that I would miscarry. So, even though I was anxious to hear back from the office, I was scared because I just didn't want to hear any bad news. So, finally the nurse is on the other end of the receiver and all I heard was "Sorry, Mrs. Kinsey; but . . . ." That is the last thing I hear before I lost grip of the phone and tears just gushed. My coworker happened to come in and witness the meltdown. She immediately scooped me up in her arms and let me grieve. That day, I grieved for not only my baby, I grieved for myself. I realized that I no longer had the strength I needed to go on. But, as much as I had to die to that present, I died to my dreams of the future. I knew that day; my mission to get pregnant was over, because how could I give life when I didn't have life? This time, I knew that I needed more than a break from the treatments; I needed for this journey to end; even if it was without my baby. I was completely depleted. I had nothing left.

After awhile, I stopped crying and then the hard part began. It was time for me to face the strongholds that kept me bonded and they went far beyond infertility issues. I sat for hours talking to my co worker about what has transpired of my life. The thing that sticks out the most about this specific experience was her gentleness. I felt that she could sense my urgency for restoration. She knew that I was holding on by a shred, and all she did was listen and literally hold both my hands. After I finished, she kindly said, "I know a doctor that can help you, because she helped me". At that very moment I knew that I needed a whole village to raise me out of this turmoil. I think the reason that I was so willing to accept her advice, versus my mother's advice for a psychologist, was because she used compassion to help guide me. I did not feel judged, she used herself to relate to me by saying, "I was at a dark space similar to your self and I needed help to get out". That statement brought down all my defenses, and made me face the honest truth; that I could no longer do this thing by myself. I could not longer think that all I needed was a break and I could go right back in to the same routine.

Shortly after the encounter with my co worker, I started using psychotherapy as a tool to rebuild my confidence. I want to share some words with you that are words I was taught during this time and that I live by now. I pray that during your road through infertility or any hardship that you too can use these words to live by. One question that the therapist asked me after I spent an hour talking; or rather crying about just how much I wanted a baby and believed that it would never happen; she asked one questioned that changed my life. It was the question that completely allowed me to look at this journey in another light. She asked me, "So what happens if you never have a baby?" The question stopped me in my tracks because even though that was my biggest fear; I wasn't ready to articulate it. Of course by this part of my journey I had asked myself that question silently, but never out loud, because, saying it out loud really made it true. I didn't want to ever think that I would never have a family. So, I wept at the question and nervously paced the floor back and forth in my mind to avoid it. I must have sat there for five minutes in total panic before I looked in her eyes and realized that she really wanted me to answer the question and that I wasn't going to leave without her getting that answer. I needed that answer. I did not need her and she knew that. I think that's why she sat there patiently waiting for it. So, I hesitantly stated, "I guess I would just have to live". Our eyes stayed glued to one another and we sat there in silence for seconds. Tears swelled up in my eyes because I knew I just made a powerful statement. No matter what happened; wasn't going to happen; or will happen on this journey to motherhood, I had to live. I had to define myself outside of being a mother. I had to come to terms that I must shoot for my other dreams because it was no way I was going to just lay down and die because I could not give birth to a child. I already resided in a dead place and it was no way I would allow myself to be put back in that space. So, I'm sitting on the couch and the therapist passed me a box of tissues because I was crying inconsolably and that was okay. I knew that I needed to do that; I needed to grieve for the things that I had lost to that point. I had to grieve my dreams that had to be put on hold or even gone. I had to grieve the past experiences that have put in such a desperate and hurt space. Lastly, I had to grieve the fact that I may never become a mother. The last thing that I wanted to contemplate was how my life would be without the children that I desired. But, even though the therapist's tactics and questions were necessary; apart of me just couldn't cope with that fact; it definitely hit me right in the gut. So, I just continued to let my answer marinate and then she asked me to repeat what I just said, I guess to reintegrate my recent conviction. I played along and I was surprised that the words came out as effortlessly as they did, "I have to live". Now, that my mouth was finally verbalizing this truth, my head and heart was beginning to get on board. It was also in that very moment that I realized that I was strong enough to deal with any outcome of this journey; I realized that fear held me back from the strength that I needed so desperately to cling on to. Now, I will never lie and say that in this moment I accepted that I would never bare a child; that was not the case. I just accepted the fact that it was a possibility that it might not happen for me and that if that was the case; I need to find contentment in the other aspects of my life. The lesson learned was that I confronted a fear and gave myself permission to contemplate other outcomes of this journey; whether it be more treatments; adoption; or just diving full force in my marriage and career. It was time to rationalize that it was very possible that this journey was over and not going to end up with me carrying a baby to term and snuggling my face up against my baby's face upon its arrival. It was time to deliberate just how to create a life for myself outside of trying to become a mother. There were so many aspects of my life that I completely shut down because my mission was to get pregnant and nothing took president over that. That very day, I left the therapist's office with a new attitude towards myself and life. I had new words to live by and it was, "TO LIVE"! I left out of there with a renewed spirit about living life. It had been so long since I wanted to live outside of my own personal pity party. I wanted to be apart of society again! I wanted to open myself up to relationships and love again. My ministry has always been there to listen, encourage, and empower people; I wanted to live my life again in obedience to God.

So ladies, if I don't give you anything else with this chapter, let me give you a way out of the cloudiness that infertility plants in your brain. I don't want you to forget yourself in the process. We get caught up with daily injections and monitoring that we forget to live outside of that world. Even if you feel like you don't want to step back from the process like I had do; get yourself involved with something other than obsessing with getting pregnant. Take the time to enjoy the night air on your skin and the sweet dew on the flowers. Take time to appreciate the simplicity of life y taking long strolls hand in hand with your mate or having personal; in depth conversations with new people, who possess different perspectives in life. Ladies, no matter how crippling the pain gets, remember to feel the other amusements of life. Remember to cherish the moments that create life long memories. I need for you to find what feeds your spirit and keep you encouraged.

My search for bliss was in full gear. I found it in therapy, acupuncture, and good friends. I remember the first time I met my acupuncturist and she felt my shoulders. She told me that she had never met a woman whose muscles were so tense; she said they felt like hard knots the size of golf balls. I wore my stress on my sleeves, face, and body; literally. Shortly after the acupuncturist prepped me for the session and started, I fell asleep and could heard my own self snore! It was like an out-of-body experience, here I was asleep on this table with needles sticking everywhere but yet, I could see and hear myself asleep and snoring. The constant; subtle noise kept waking me out of the relaxation; now you know that was a whole lot of stress trying to escape my body! Another saving grace on this part of the journey was my friends; who lend an ear above anything else. They patiently listened as I whined about being a mother. But, no matter how many times I ranted and raved on the same subject, I had their ears every time. My friends became my family. I can't express to you how important it is to surround yourself with people who sincerely love you and support your efforts; even if they don't understand or agree. Criticism for wanting to start a family with your husband/ significant other is judgmental and heartless. How could something so natural and beautiful, not be worth fighting for. So, if someone can not understand your pure desires in wanting a child, it's important that you remove yourself from their advances; because at your vulnerable state, that could be earth shattering for your feelings. You don't need someone beating you upside your head with thoughtless opinions and comments. See, people think they are justified in articulating their harsh opinions, no matter how much their words damage other people. The truth is, speaking your mind to the point where you emotionally kill someone is wrong and sinful, and the word of God speaks on how we can speak life and death with our tongues. It speaks on being your brother's keeper, not tearing down your brother when they are already lying on the floor. Truthfully, the old saying never dies, "Misery loves company." See, when people don't want you to advance in life because their life is stagnant; they make you feel guilty or foolish to want to better and farther your life. And ladies, that is why it is vital to keep people with good and sincere intentions around you. It is vital, so that you can keep an enlightened and encouraged heart while you brave the road of infertility.

If I could give you more words to live by while marching through this journey, it is to always go with your gut. Like, I mentioned earlier, it's easy to get caught up in other people's opinions about your situations when you are weak. But honestly, I went against theories, facts, and the opinions of others all of the time in this journey. I refused to lose focus of what my heart wanted, even when my head told me to stop. At one point my gut told me to stop; and I did just that! Matter of fact, if I listened to what people said about my situation, I would be unable to write this love letter to you and outline it with the faith that helped me get to the end of it. So, let me give you a pep talk that no one could give me because they couldn't see things the way you and I are able to. So, if your gut is telling you to stop or take a break or if you have to take a long hiatus, do so. That turned out to be vital to my survival going through this journey and it gave me what I needed to restart my walk. My point for this chapter is to help you find your own way to start living outside of this very difficult journey and to give you words to live by and the most important word of the all; is to, LIVE!

Chapter 4

A Miracle Unfolds

A Miracle So Sweet

Something so sweet
And so divinely orchestrated
Heavenly written
Has been etched into my life's book
And the joy of it leaves this giddiness inside my stomach
A tickle in my voice
The light in my eyes are restored
The hue of my skin is brightened
And all I can see is love
Love so pure and without intent
It only wants me to embrace it
To take it within myself without fear or boundary
All I want to do is accept it
Cherish it as if my very breath depended on it
Something so sweet
And so divinely orchestrated
Heavenly written
Has been permanently etched into my life's book

A miracle is an event that exceeds the known laws of nature and science. Usually an act of God done through human agents.

The word miracle defines this final leg of this expedition. Up until this point, I have traveled from a dark hole to places where I could allow the warmth of the sunshine on my face. I have traveled over and through confusion, anger, mental torture, spiritual warfare, false hopes, low self esteem, minimal self worth, sadness, depression, suicidal thoughts, and just plan ole weariness. I have walked, ran, powered walked, jogged, sprinted, and skipped through this journey to get close to the finish line! This is the most exciting part of the process in writing this book. Not only, do I pray this stage of the journey gives you hope to keep pressing on; I want you to get one important thing. I want you to know that God hears and see the tears and cries that you have shed throughout your own individual plights. I want you to know that our heavenly father is still in the business of giving us the things that our hearts desire; whether it's a baby, job opportunity, career move, life changing purpose, or just a total healing; God wants to bless you. I sincerely from the bottom of my heart want you to get that this plight is not a punishment; it's a test. It's a test of your ability to really exercise your faith and trusting God long enough to speak to you through your situation. He wants to expand you and give you the tools you need to be able to share with the next person; so that they may not have to go through the same lessons you fought through. You can give someone a chance to live to their full potential without going through some of the hardships that you had to journey through to get yours. God wants to help you in spite of your thoughts.

The way the end of the journey approaches me is nothing short of miraculous. I need you to watch just how God moved in an impossible situation and how this story is brought full circle. Now remember, when I shared earlier in this book about the hope chest I started that I filled a with baby stuff after a dream I had, where I was holding a light complexioned baby girl with black, curly hair. Well, turns out that this hope chest was preparing me for my truth, but not on the time table that I set out for myself.

It seemed that getting pregnant was impossible. I figured that since my dreams and hope chest was just a figure of my imagination, it was time to look at the facts, so my husband and I started looking into other options. Since we had tried all the methods for reproducing on our own, we settled on adoption. We contemplated a surrogate, but my heart could not come to the grips of another woman carrying my baby. Another woman gets to watch her tummy grow and feel the movement of our baby. Its wasn't fair that my husband couldn't turn over in the middle of the night and rub my tummy or get irritated when I insisted on him making a midnight run to the market for pickles and ice cream. So given all our reservations with surrogacy, we opted for adoption. We just didn't want the feeling of loosing another thing, we had already lost three pregnancies and we didn't want to loose the aspect of experiencing our pregnancy first handed. So, the story takes an unusual twist, God spoke to me one day in a department store while I was shopping through baby cloths. My husband and I were halfway through the process of adopting, so I felt safe enough to pull my hope chest back out and start putting more things in my hope chest. Even though I always dreamed of being pregnant and expecting a baby; I finally accepted that I didn't have to birth a child to be a mother. So, I'm shopping for baby girl clothing because I still felt like the dream of me having this little girl would still be manifested, but now it would be through adoption. I'm filling my cart up with pink thrills; something spoke so loud and clear to buy infant boys cloths for the specific age range of 6-9 months. I begin questioning God on why would I do such a thing, I put on my adoptions papers that we were open for a little girl . . . . not a boy. But, I realized it was time to open my heart to loving any child in need of a mother. I brought those clothes and tucked them safely in my hope chest.

Two months after my department store revelation, my husband and I finished our home study and all the paperwork, I even changed our eligibility with the gender and opened our home to any infant. Our adoption worker tried her hardest to change our age range from infancy to toddler/older children; but I would not budge with that. I knew that the need for older kids to be placed in a home was great; my heart just wanted to experience the baby stage of a child's development. My worker even went as far as to say that if we refuse to change our age eligibility; we would be waiting two years for a baby. My gut told me to act strong on my convictions, that we would receive a baby and I was willing to wait two years if needed because at this time, I had already waited over five years. So, we finished up the first part of the adoption process, and now we are just waiting for our baby. Even though I knew that the worker said we would be waiting for two years, I knew it wouldn't be that long. The miracle is that it didn't take two years, it only took two months! Yes, you read it right, I knew it would probably happen before that two year mark, but never did we imagine it happening that quickly. My worker called us on a Wednesday and told me that she had an available six month old baby boy who was exposed to four different types of drugs during his gestation. Without hesitation, I said, "When can I expect my son?" I sure wasn't prepared for the answer. She replied, "Friday". I said," Well today is Wednesday and they are calling for the biggest snowstorm in Baltimore since 1996". She assured me that she knew that and that they would try to place him before the snowstorm came. We were so excited and anxious to meet our son and I had everything that a mother would need for her six month old right in my HOPE CHEST. Now, not only was the length of time miraculous in our situation, our son was not even suppose to be available for adoption. He was already in a good home; but his foster home was not an adoptive home. Since, my worker and my son's social worker are good friends and our worker knew how adamant we were to have an infant; she was quick to recommend my husband and me to her colleague. I couldn't help but just sit back and smile because this situation solidified my hope chest and the direction that God gave me with what to put in it. My hope chest wasn't crazy; God was just preparing me for what he was to have me do . . . . on his time! So, over the next few months after my son arrived; my family of three was so happy. Everyday my husband and I took full advantage of the newfound love that our household just received. We both were so crazy about him and he fell in love with us just as quickly and equally,

I really felt content. But, I did not feel complete yet. I thought that I would feel cheated because I didn't get the opportunity to birth him, but I felt just as connected with him as if I did give birth to him. I believed that it would take time to get in tune with him and to get the mother/ son bond established. The truth is the first time I picked my son up, took his snow suit off and lifted his hat to peak into his eyes; it was instant. He smiled at me as if he was saying, "Mommy, What took you so long to get here?" The way he reached out to me when I came into the room, and him gripping my finger when I feed him; made our connection solid and unbreakable.

Even though things were going so well, those gut feeling started to creep back in. My husband and I had one more IVF available to us, but after the last miscarriage we agreed not to try anything soon. Something in me was telling me it was time. And I could not shake the feeling. So, I started on my husband, who was hesitant at first. He hit me with the, "Honey, the last miscarriage took too much out of you and we both agreed that we would give it time" line. He reminded me that we had a son to give our time and energy to and that it would not be fair to bring him along on that emotional roll coaster. Even though, I knew he was right, I could not shake the feeling. I knew it was time to try, I knew that it was time to meet that little girl in my dreams. After weeks of nagging and almost bullying my husband to agree to the last IVF; my efforts paid off. I finally convinced my husband to get on board. Here I was, with all my dreams and aspirations in tow. I was so excited and the day I called to start our new cycle, the unthinkable happens. My whole world gets crushed in one minute and one phone call. And, most importantly our plans to start our new IVF cycle threatened to be derailed . . . . permanently.

It was Palm Sunday and my mother planned a dinner at my home. The television in our living room was broke and my husband was the only one who could fix it. At the time he was working and only had two hours left on his shift, but I was persistent in asking him to run home to fix it because our company was on their way for dinner shortly. So, he agreed to come and was there within fifteen minutes. He fixed the television and even spared a couple minutes to take pictures and goof around with me and our son before he left. So, as he walked out he asked me for the keys to our brand new SUV. I remember teasing him saying that he only wanted to take it to show it off, but I went to get the keys anyway. Six months prior we were in a bad car accident that by an act of God; our lives were spared. So, I knew it felt good for him to be able to buy a new SUV because of his guilt with the previous accident leaving me with a broken bone in my spine. So, I gave him the keys and kissed him goodbye. As soon as he pulled off, I had this gut wrenching feeling out the pit of my stomach, I was so mad that even though I knew I should have drove him back to work; I did not. I mean, he told me he wasn't tired and could handle the short drive, I knew better. Five minutes later I received a phone call that proved that my intuition was right. My husband voice was on the other end and it was shaky and disoriented. I just knew what happened, I knew that life as we knew it was about to change. My husband spoke those dreadful words as soon as I said hello, "Dani, I have been in an accident", He told me his location and it just went silent. I screamed his name several times without a response and my heart sunk down to my feet, I feared the worst. Even though he is an epileptic, I felt like it was more than a seizure and I just couldn't phantom that the man I love was going to leave me for good. So, by now I'm in the car with my dad racing to the crash scene and I'm still screaming for my husband to answer me, I was so desperate just to her a whisper of his voice. I needed to know he was still alive. How could the man that unselfishly just came to my rescue to help me prepare for a family dinner be gone? How more selfish could I been for asking him to come home after a long work day, when he was so tired because he started picking up more shifts at work to support our new family? We had just got to a wonderful space in our marriage and had became the parents that we so desperately wanted to be; for everything to be taken away now. On top of that he takes so many medications just to keep the epilepsy under control, and plus the drugs keep him sleepy. I shouldn't have called him to come home for a dumb television set that could have been replaced. I could of least road him back to work, instead of entertaining my company. I felt so stupid and beyond guilty, how could I ever live with myself if something was to happen to him? I was as good as dead if that was my reality. A voice came through the phone and it felt like salvation. It wasn't my husband's voice, but a bystander who was helping the victims of the accident. The man assured me that my husband was indeed still alive, but was in no condition to hold a conversation. I quickly told the man he had seizures, just to prepare someone if he was to go into one. My father and I had arrived at the scene and it looked like World War 1. The whole road was blocked, so I had to run out the vehicle to run towards the scene. I franticly ran and my husband and our two week old vehicle was no where in sight, all I seen was three other cars wrecked. One car even has the jars of life trying to free a woman. In another car, a woman was slumped over the steering wheel, lifelessly. My heart just dropped and I ran until I seen my husband. There he was, lying on the ground on top of the disconnected tire with blood pulling from his head. I remember just darting down in a pool of burnt tire and glass to scoop him up. Miraculously, he was responsive and the blood that was pulling from his head was a bad scrape. So, I just cradled him and let him know that everything was going to be okay. All he kept saying was, "Dani, I killed someone, I just want to die." Those words pierced me like a dagger through my heart. He just kept shaking and saying those words. No matter how much I reassured him that no one was dead as result of the accident, his mind believed different. By God's unwavering grace, my husband along with the victims in the three other vehicles was not badly hurt. The most serious injury was a fractured elbow, not to discredit the psychological and emotional distress of every victim. Here we was, once again capture in yet another miracle. My husband just survived a second brutal head on collision. I can't describe the elation that I felt to be able to hold my husband in my arms that night, if I didn't appreciate him before; I did then. For days following the accident, all I could do was look at the pictures my husband took with my son and I right before he took back off to work. The thing that obsessed my mental process was that it could have very well been the last time that we were together as a family. As much as I try to focus on the positive, I just couldn't get over the reality that one day that would be my reality because it is everyone's reality, we all are not here to stay; it's funny how life has a way of making you face your fears. Just like how the therapist made me face the fear of never being a mother. Well, my next fear was about to be confronted; there was no way we could move forward on our plans to start our next and final Invitro fertilization procedure. During the next couple of weeks, I didn't even mention the procedure to my husband. After all he had been through, I knew he was struggling. Not only did he have to physically heal, he had to come to grips with the fact that he could no longer drive. Now, I understand you might think it's not a big thing that he can't drive; he escaped with his life. Well the truth is because he had epilepsy, technically he wasn't suppose to drive or live a full life. But, he was able to exceed society's expectations and drive, plus work a full time job. It wasn't good enough for my husband to sit home and collect social security; he grew into a man with pride. He fought everyday to work and provide for his family and now the law and his health was taking that from him. Even though this was a hard pill to swallow; I tried my best to make my husband feel like he was a man. But, no band aid can cover up the scar of a man's pride and the inability of providing for his family is taken away. I even swallowed my fears just to make him feel confident, even though I was scared because the blunt of the responsibilities were going to be mine again. During this time, the communication between my husband and I dwindled down to none. His pain had cost him to shut down again and push me away and there was nothing I could do about it.

It was six weeks after the accident and out of no where my husband questioned me about the procedure. In amazement, but without hesitation I spilled my desires to move forward. Looking back at that time, I really think we both just wanted to feel like we weren't losing yet another thing. The procedure went smoothly and we found ourselves waiting for our nurse to call back with the results of our pregnancy test. The nurse gave us the best news we could ask for at the time, we were pregnant. Although we were happy, we've been there before; we just wanted to know if the pregnancy was viable and healthy. Our joy was shortened because the next blood test showed that the numbers were not doubling and indicated another failed pregnancy. But, this time was different; my numbers were constantly going up, but just not doubling like they typically should. The doctors urged me to abort the embryo because my HSG levels refusing to completely double meant tragedy and that the pregnancy was not viable or healthy. I wasn't convinced that the pregnancy was doomed, so I asked for an ultrasound. I thought that maybe this would be my miracle and although my levels were doing something strange; the ultrasound would reveal a baby with a strong heartbeat. I had no such luck; it only revealed an empty sac without a heartbeat. Although this was true, my HSG levels kept rising and the entire time the doctor said was that it is not unlikely that you will miscarry. I don't know if I was just trying to hold on to the pregnancy, afraid of experiencing the pain again or was it God telling me to fight for this baby. I decided to fight and believe me; I came to the ring ready to win. One month had gone by and by now the fertility clinic put an A.P.B out on me. They left me message after message, asking me to come in and abort because the pregnancy was not viable and that I could get sick with the tissue inside of me. I was determined not to go that route. I knew that even if this pregnancy was over, I would let it dispel naturally just like the previous ones. I wasn't going to play God, I told him that if this pregnancy was indeed detrimental to me or the baby; to take it away. Then, one night while I was sleep; I felt a gush. I didn't even have to check, I knew it was blood. Something in me died that night. Here I was, excited because I thought I beat all odds and proved those doctors wrong. I got up, cleaned up and accepted that I had another angel looking over us. Of course, my husband and I were devastated; but the difference this time was that we had a family now and we put all our energy into raising our son. I still would cry at night, but I knew God knew best. I did feel like I lost my little girl that I seen in my dreams; but I was determined not to make my son take the loss. He deserved a happy mother, so I refused to succumb to the depression that plagued me last time. After I cried my heart out for a week after the bleeding; I pushed on. I got back in our routine and did my best to push forward. I figured since I had the bleeding, which wasn't a full period, that I miscarried and God did what I asked. I asked him to allow me to miscarry naturally without medical intervention if it had to happen.

A few more weeks past and sadness was still looming, but there was more than sadness looming because my health was taking a toll. I thought that maybe depression was creeping in and making me fell ill. Eventually, I had to make a trip to the emergency room because my throat was so sore, I couldn't hardly swallow. I remember being so angry driving to the ER, I couldn't believe that everything that has transpired, from my husband's car accident leaving him feeling depressed and without a license to the miscarriage. I felt myself asking God, "Haven't I paid enough?" Now, I have to go to the ER and God knows I was in no condition to hear anymore bad news. So, I dropped my son off to my mother's house and my husband and I headed to the hospital. I found myself sitting in the cold hospital room, which was cold and impersonal. As my husband and I sat waiting for the results of my blood test, I got this headache that thumped as hard as my heartbeat. Just thinking about all the things that could have been wrong had me terrified, by the time the doctor came in I'd convinced myself that I had cancer. It wasn't cancer, the doctored said, "You are pregnant". He said it looked like I was in the first trimester because of my hormone levels and told me to follow up with my OB/GYN. I know what you're thinking; my husband and I should have been overjoyed with that news. We weren't because we been there before. We just knew that my levels didn't go all the way down from my recent miscarriage and I probably made a mistake by not going to fully dispel of the pregnancy. Apart of me was relieved that I didn't have a major health crisis, but the other part of me was beginning the grieving process all over again. Here I was, facing the reality that I had to go to the doctors and deal with a situation that I thought met its conclusion. The ride home from the ER was a quiet one. I didn't call my OBGYN the next day. I just didn't want to deal with the situation and be reminded that my pregnancy did not work out; but I wasn't ready for the new tidal wave that was rolling in.

A week or so after the emergency room event, my husband got a phone call that his father had died. The plan was for him not to have a funeral and to be cremated; so his loved ones had to hurry to the funeral home to say their goodbyes. We didn't even have time to process the information, let alone wrap our heads around the fact that this was really happening. But, my husband put on a brave face and we went to say our goodbyes. I can remember my husband walking out of the room where his father's body laid after saying his final goodbyes; he said nothing. He just fell in his mother's arms and cried; I have never seen him that emotional before. I remember asking God to bring my husband some joy because of how heartbreaking it was for him to loose a father and baby so close to one another. I remember the old saying, "When someone dies, someone is about to be born", and I told my husband that it would be a miracle if your dad can help push a baby our way. My husband gave me a half of a smile, indicating that he stilled had hope for the situation. I finally got the courage to call my OBGYN and schedule an appointment. I did not tell her anything about the failed in-vitro fertilization procedure, I just told her that I got a positive pregnancy test and wanted to confirm it; I didn't want her to be bias and agree with the fertility specialist and abort the baby. She knew my history of difficult pregnancies and didn't waste anytime; my appointment was for the next morning. I went to take my blood test and when she got the results she called and confirmed that it was positive. I couldn't believe it, it was a little over three months since the ultrasound showed an empty sac without a heartbeat. It was weeks after my ER visit and my test was positive. She told me my HSG level was 30,000 and she was going to retest it in two days and they should have doubled. So, I went back and my number was 37,000, not 60,000, she told me that the pregnancy was not vital. I was devastated and felt so stupid for getting my hopes up. She wanted to schedule an ultrasound to see exactly what was inside my uterus, so she could see what methods were available to dispel of the fetus.

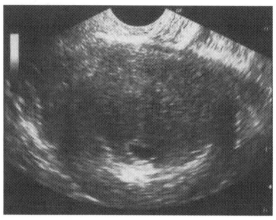

This is when my baby was considered a miscarriage. There was obviously no embryo in the sac, nor heartbeat.

The day of my ultrasound, I was very calm. Even though I was nervous to see what was on the inside of my uterus; I knew I had to be responsible and take care of my health. Most importantly, it was time to put this thing to bed; I had to stop clinging on to the hope of a miracle taking place and the pregnancy actually working out. So, I dropped my husband off at work and headed to my appointment. I made it up in my mind that it wasn't the end to a horrible experience but a beginning to the rest of my life. I mean, I had a lot to be happy about. My husband who really loves and adores me; I had a brand new son; and I was finishing up my second book of poetry. I remember everything I learned in my counseling sessions; I had to LIVE and that's all I wanted to do. I found myself in a normal position, laying on the medical table with my feet on the stir ups. The nurse came in and asked me when my last period was. I told her about three months ago and she proceeded to put the warm jelly like substance on my belly. At that very moment, all my nerves and fear begin flooding my brain. I thought I was handling everything so well, I was thinking it was a mistake to come alone. My eyes were glued shut, I wasn't ready to see what was inside of me; but I soon heard it. It was the most beautiful noise I ever heard; it was my baby's heartbeat. Yes, I said it! It was my baby's heartbeat. I quickly opened my eyes and I saw my baby flipping all around. I couldn't believe that I was staring at the same baby, who I was told was not vital. It was the same baby that was just an empty sac three months prior. My baby was alive. I saw a head, body, feet, and arms. I had a human being residing in my body and all I could do was praise God. Yes, I did! I just thanked him over and over again as tears poured like a thunderstorm. The nurse sat there and let me have my moment. After, I finished she asked me if was okay and I responded, "You don't understand, they told me that my baby was not alive". I saw the baby with my own eyes. There was no baby or heartbeat! She assured me that my baby was very well alive and that I could be expecting him or her in a little less than six months. The nurse then went to get the doctor and as soon as the door shut; I called my husband at work. He was in total shock and couldn't believe what I was telling him and before we hung up I said, "Your father helped pushed his grandchild through". He simply responded, "Yep". I was so thrilled to hear the giddiness in my husband voice because I haven't heard it since his accident and I knew he was silently thanking his dad; his heavenly father and biological one. The doctor came in and talked to me for an hour, but I hardly remember the details! I was so elated and on cloud nine; I don't even remember the ride home. I was overtaken with disbelief, gratefulness, and joy for what was going on inside of me. I knew I wasn't crazy, and I knew what God has promised me. I knew at that very moment that my hope chest was only to prepare me for what was destined to happen. I felt justified. The "little girl" in me wanted to stick my tongue out to all the people who told me that I was crazy, obsessed, and wasn't destined to have children. I wanted to scream "I told you so" to the people who told me that it wasn't my time and that I should give up. But, I reveled in silence because I didn't have to say those things because God was showing those things . . . . to all the people who didn't believe, or those who found joy in my misery. Restoration was staring me in my eyes.

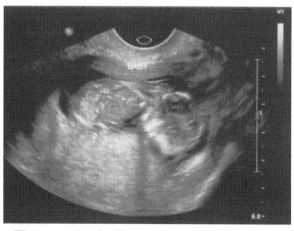

Three months after I was told that my baby was not vital and I needed to have an abortion. As you can see, that baby is formed and flipped upside down! The heart was strong and steady!

Chapter 5

Challenged Restoration

Today

Today is different I feel the warmth of the sun on my
cheek
I smile because I can smell God's grace with every wind
that blows
My spirit feels playful
I'm filled with soft whispers of laughter
My hearts want to love in abundance
These feelings are a bit surreal
Feels like I'm living inside my dreams today
My soul is satisfied. It sits like a belly full and content
I know beauty today
And its sight is far more angelic as the glow that
shadows an angel's face
Today is different
Like nothing I have seen before
And like something I will never see again

(Jeremiah 30:17 58) "For I will restore health to you, and your wounds I will heal, declares the Lord!"

*R*estoration is the replacement or giving back of something lost; stolen

This chapter mirrors the restoration of everything which was lost in this journey. In these final steps in my voyage; God starts to renew my faith and strength through the miracle of carrying life inside my body. For seven years, I have waited for the revelation of my dreams, hopes, and prayers. In those seven years at various stops and twists throughout this journey; I lost faith, strength, peace, relationships, patience, and self worth and now all of that was being replenished.

I named the chapter, "Challenged Restoration" because my redemption and restoration came at a challenge and a hefty price. Although, I spent sevens years in turmoil and the price of my oil was down right expensive; I was not done paying for it. Even though I was on my way to what a woman suffering in infertility dreams of; it came with its own set of challenges. I know what you must be thinking: How could she spend all this time towards the goal of achieving a healthy pregnancy and have issues when she arrived there? And even though I had a high risk pregnancy due to specific medical conditions of mine; the personal issues seem to out weigh it all. Please don't think for one moment that I was not over the moon with excitement that my destiny was being fulfilled, but I had no idea that I was going to lose as much as I was set to gain.

One of the biggest and most devastating obstacles of this time was the complete breakdown of my family's structure, communication, and inner personal relationships. The very same family and friends, that has known my struggles from the beginning and have watched apart of my spirit die from the previous lost; had no interest or joy in the miracle that was growing inside of me. Yes, they had their reservations about my decision to seek medical help with my infertility, but never would I except them to disregard me when I finally got to the place where my dreams resided. It was funny that when I was down and out, everyone flocked to my misery, but as soon as the underdog threatened to put everyone under me, a problem arose. I referred to myself as the underdog, simply because I was bluntly told that I was the underdog when I confronted a family member about the hurt I had because of the family abandoning gestures towards me. Even though their logic made perfect sense, how could I be the underdog when I had a decent life. I thought an underdog had little to nothing. I thought the underdog was more unlikely to succeed. I may not have had all the material possessions of some people, but I had a marriage; education; and children. That comment about me being the underdog floored me and only validated my questions about my family's detachment from my life and everything that was going on in it. As long as everyone felt above me and that their life mirrored a reflection that wasn't as devastating as mine; I was their priority. But, my heart still didn't want to believe that truth and questions still flooded my thought process. How could they watch me walk through hell and not rejoice in this miraculous blessing? How could they run my name through the dirt as if we were not in love at one time? How could they not rejoice with me, when I have rejoiced in all their victories and accomplishments? I had all these questions with an answer that I refused to believe; and that was that they just were not happy for me. They let their own pain get in the way of celebrating this miracle with me and that left me devastated. I still didn't give into that truth so easily and I even gave my family the benefit of doubt and convinced myself that my hormones were to blame. I was pregnant and chasing around a one year old! Maybe I was just being too sensitive and expecting too much, but all suspensions came to an abrupt end on the day of my son's first birthday party.

It was the hottest day of the summer, over 100 degrees. But in spite of all of that, I was overjoyed because I had spent the last three months planning a wonderful "pool party/ island extravaganza", for my son's first birthday party. I had three pools, blowup tropical trees, beach pails filled with candy, water slides, water balloons, beach toys, a palm tree shaped piñata, and enough food to feed an army! It was a bit over the top, but I just felt like my son deserved it. He has brought our household so much fun and joy and the least I could do was show off for his birthday; he deserved so much more. With all of the excitement involved in my progressive pregnancy, I wanted it to be about him until the baby's arrival. So, given my happy mood, there was nothing that could have altered it . . . . so I thought. I hosted the party at my relative's house, even though I had my reservations; I was hopeful that this joyful occasion would unite us rather than bring more damage towards the breaking down of our structure. My family did not exist inside of harmony that day and I found myself almost in a physical altercation with my relative over emotions and foolishery. The only reason it turned physical because for so long we have allowed our silence to keep our feelings pressed down. All we needed was communication and to abandon our pride.

But, we were incapable of doing that at the present time. As disgusted as I was with our total disregard for each other's feelings and not valuing the baby that I finally was blessed to carry; I was more disgusted with myself for responding to their antics. Here I was, finally pregnant and I had the nerve to jeopardize the health of my unborn child because of someone's ignorance and malicious intent. I had a choice to remove myself from the situation; I decided that I will longer be apart of the problem. As many families, my family have an issue with back biting and mistreating one another and I had enough with it. I could no longer pretend that I wanted to live that way; I wanted to find a place of peace, truth, and happiness. The truth was I am a product of my environment, but that day I decided to be the exception. I made up in my mind in those very emotionally struggling moments that I would no longer be their punching bag; I no longer would be the person that they helped shaped, that loved and reveled in back stabbing and drama. This time was meant to be precious. I was preparing to give birth. I needed to only be involved in that. I dried my tears and realized that my family structured had changed and my devotion was due to my husband, son, and the baby that was in my belly.

Over the following months after the fight with my family, I learned how to fully depend on my husband. Given that my support system was so tiny, he was definitely at the center of it. Looking back in hindsight, my pregnancy and the breakdown of my extended family and my parents really strengthened my marriage. For the first time in our marriage, my husband became the strength in it. Since the beginning of our relationship, I took on the load and became the strength in the relationship. Even though eventually I resented him for it, I had to own my part in the situation. Why should he be the dominate one when I have taken that from him? It was more than overdue and relieving to give that role back to the leader of our household. It brought a whole new level of honor and respect to our relationship. The new transition in our new found relationship seemed to be what we needed to marveled in this pregnancy. I remember sitting up at night time after we put our son to bed, just talking about our futures and the dream of giving our children a wonderful childhood. We both just had a new zeal for life and we both wanted to make the very best out of it. The night of that very hopeful and intimate conversation, we just let each other dream aloud. Even though the breakdown of my family was definite, I was so appreciative of the new family that God gave me and I had nothing but gratitude for that truth. My husband and I became like the giddy teenagers we once was when we fell in love. Even though things were not perfect, we enjoyed this newfound happiness and all our free time was filled with laughter and playfulness. Before we formerly found out our unborn child gender, guessing what our unborn child's gender was definitely the source of our playfulness. My husband and I was approaching week 19 of my pregnancy and we had an appointment to find out the gender of the baby. I knew in my heart the sex, but my husband was hanging on for dear life to hear . . . . it's a boy! I knew that God was completing the revelation of that repeated dream that I had since I was eighteen, so when the lady said it was a girl; I was not surprised at all. My husband got over it really quick and we both went in full baby mode with preparing for our baby girl. That same day my little family of three went to start our baby register to prepare for our family of four! Even though it was such a humbling and exciting time, our dreams were about to become our nightmare.

It was week 25 of my pregnancy and a gush of water woke me up out my sleep, My first initial reaction was that I urinated on myself; which is not uncommon in the second trimester of pregnancy. So, I made my way to the bathroom and cleaned myself up and climbed back in bed. But, before I could close my eyes to go back to dreamland; another gush pulled out. I immediately hopped up and used my hands to feel for what came out and I was praying to God it wasn't blood. I finally got to the point in the pregnancy where I wasn't scared that I was going to lose my baby; and here I was thinking I was having a late term miscarriage. To my surprise, it was a white gel-like substance and I knew right away that it was my mucus plug. I knew it was way too early for that and I immediately woke my husband up and we rushed straight to the emergency room. Everything was going through my mind on the ride over to the hospital, I was petrified with the fact I was going into early labor. What would happen to my baby? I was barely six months.

I arrived at the emergency room and was rushed straight to the maternity ward. My worse fears were being manifested right before my eyes. The doctor checked me and confirmed that I was in labor and my water did indeed break. All I could do was cry; I just didn't understand what could go so horribly wrong so quickly; in spite of how the pregnancy began; it had been uneventful until now. I started playing the blame game with myself, maybe this was my fault. I mean maybe I ate too much salt, I was obsessed with pickles? Maybe it was the time I made love with my husband after the doctor told me to withstand until she said so, just for precautionary reasons. Maybe it was me doing too much; I was constantly on the go. Maybe it was letting the stress and strain on the demise of my relationship with my family. It wasn't until the doctor interrupted my thoughts with, 'Mrs. Kinsey, I know this is not the ideal situation, but hope is not lost". The doctor assured me that she would survive if she was to be delivered that night, but she would definitely have a long stay in the NICU and she ran the risk of having all sorts of issues that is associated with prematurity. I learned that night that medical teams will fight for a baby life as early as 23 weeks gestation and that gave me a lot of reassurance. But, as much as I was being reassured that my baby girl would live, I couldn't believe what was happening; after everything that I had already been through till that point and now I'm faced with yet another let down. Even though, the news that my baby was viable was the best news I could hear at the time; I was still very worried. The doctor did inform me that there was no way I could go home, even on bed rest because my membranes had ruptured and that would put me and the baby at risk for infection. They also informed me that gravity was my best friend, so lying flat for as long as I could to keep the baby inside would only benefit her. After a while all the medical stuff became obsolete and I couldn't understand anything. All I knew was that I was sad and angry. I was sad because I felt that my body failed my baby, which was the same feelings I struggled with through my three previous miscarriages. The anger was more potent though, I just couldn't understand why everything in my life had to be a struggle and here I was being force to suit up for one of the biggest fights I ever had to face. I won my fight against infertility and I came to win this one too. That day, September 23, 2010; allowed me to tap into strength that I didn't know I had. I always have been a strong individual, but situations like this would humble the strongest person in the world. I had one goal, and that was to get to my destiny, no matter the cost.

Ladies, I want you to read this and be ready to suit up and continue to fight through your own individual situations. I came to the ring, ready to win and I pray that you adopt that same mentality. There is no way you can get to your finish line without the "will" and "fight" to win; you have to run past the pain. I know how it feels for your lungs to turn against you and all you want is to stop running and grasp for any breath you can find; you need that same endurance to run through the hurt. Lying in that bed, unable to do anything for myself; made me appreciate life on a whole new level. I was determined to lay in that hospital bed for as long as I could, my whole focus was to get my little girl here safely and healthy. I knew that the longer I laid there and she was in my womb, gave her a better chance for a quick recovery and shorter stay in the NICU. The last thing I wanted to do was have my baby fight so hard just to survive, but I knew she was fighter because she fought through hoops already. The doctors wanted to give up on her and advise me to terminate this pregnancy earlier on and even the ultrasounds left evidence of just an empty sac. She fought through all of that and I knew that she would fight to stay here. So I put on my game face and vowed to fight with her

Even though my heart and head was in the fight; lying in a bed 24/7 will challenge anyone's mental and emotional well being. I am a very independent person, who did everything for myself and the people around me. Now I had to let people take care of me. There I was, being force to totally submit myself to a process and focus only on my physical and mental wellbeing. I couldn't hide behind my "superwoman" and take care of everything around me. The control freak that I am was going crazy and losing control. So many questions swarm my brain. Who was going to fix my son's toast exactly the way he likes it? Who was going to help my husband if he had a seizure? Who was going to give my son his favorite blanket at bedtime or understand every one of his cries? How were all the bills going to get paid? What about my job and my students at work? I had all these questions and I hated the answer. The answer was that it was all going to get done and without me. I didn't need to assist God with anything, he was totally in control. For the first time in my life, I had no control over anything. I didn't have control over my unborn baby, body, family, and sometimes even my thoughts ran away from me. That truth killed me, but I knew the sooner I accepted that; the easier it would be for me to finish the task at hand. Some days were good, some were bad, some days I was just resentful and some days I felt down right selfish. I remember one day throwing my pillows at my husband because I was so mad that he had the liberty to go downstairs and eat in the cafeteria; where as I had to eat the crappiest diabetic diet. That day

I cursed him out in front of the nurses, which was totally out of my character. I just felt so angry and so done. I was growing tired of the needles; examinations; laying flat on my back; unable to use a toilet; having people wash my body; having people assist me with my bed pan; eating tasteless food; watching the same three channels; having my sleep interrupted with taking vital signs and blood pressure in the middle of the night; doing worthless exercises because I was inactive; reading books; and writing. I was tired of it all.

The mental aspect started to play a huge toll. All I had was time to think and harp on things. Some days I would just sit in silence and look at the ceiling like I was a mental patient. I wanted to get outside my head, but how can you do that if you are confined to such a little space with limited movement. I felt myself revisiting places that I was afraid to go and I could not escape to the everyday hustle and bustle of life. I could run an errand to block the hurt and bad thoughts; but now I had to sit and deal with them. I thought about the things that led me to self destruction. I thought about the things that shaped me into this person who was tough and hard on the outside; but hurting and so weak on the inside. I thought about the things that I had done to mask the hurt or to ignore the pain all together. As freeing as it was to sit back and really analyze who I was as a person and how far I came; it was torturous. It was time for me to let go of the past and look towards my future because the finish line to this journey of infertility was drawing near. I was only moments away and I knew that my baggage had no room for my next journey.

The emotional toll that the bed rest took was more strenuous then the physical and mental aspects. I didn't spend a lot of time crying, but I do remember one day where everything just hit me. I put my faith in my pocket and just had a pity party for myself. That morning, my nurse came in and noticed that I wasn't my typical upbeat self. She asked me what was wrong, I just looked at her and started to cry. She came close and rubbed me on my head and simply said, "It's ok, you have been through hell and it's time to just release all the confusion, hurt, and frustration". That nurse saved my life that day. I'm being a little dramatic, but I didn't have much emotional support at the time. It was unrealistic to have the people, who were in my life to be there around the clock. Sure, my husband was there, but giving emotional support is not one of his strengths and the last thing I needed was a pep talk. I needed a hug, kiss, and comforting words. I needed to know that someone noticed my struggle and sacrifice. I wanted someone to give me the fuel I needed to keep doing what I had to do for my unborn daughter. I also began to wrestle again with the lack of support from my family and friends; the feelings that I had towards those strained relationships started to take center stage in my mind and also played on my emotional meltdown that day. Even though, the communication between some of my family and I had broke totally down; I was very hurt that most of them did not reach out to me at that time. In my head, I believed that no matter what was going on that they should have come to see about me. For goodness sake, my health and baby's life was in jeopardy; all bets should have been off. The lesson that I learned after being separated from my family at this crucial time was to love without an agenda and motive. I had to love them without the agenda of getting them to love and accept me. As much as I tried to deny how much I loved and wanted them despite our differences; I simply couldn't continue to do so. I had to learn in the hardest way, to except them just as they were; even if it meant bruised feelings and egos. I had to learn to love them without expecting what I desired from them in return. I learned to love without expectations and selfishness. That comfort from the nurse that day definitely made me feel better about everything that was going on throughout my emotions and it gave me a second wind. Even, though I caught my second wind; it didn't allow me to run much longer because nineteen days after my water broke . . . . it was time. My power walk was becoming a fast sprint to the finish line to this journey.

It happened all so fast, but all so slow at the same time! It was 5:30am and time for my daily baby's routine monitoring when I felt two horrific cramps in my vagina. I knew something was not right. I immediately called the nurse and she quickly put me on the monitor to see if the baby was okay. I was relieved to see that the baby was fine and no contractions were visible on the monitor. I blew a sign of relief and settled back into my usual position on my back. Surprisingly, the nurse called for the doctor and I immediately asked her what was wrong because nothing was unusual about the monitoring. The nurse reassured me that things were okay, she just wanted to make sure because I never complained of any cramping. Well, her intuition was right because when the doctor checked, I was 100% effaced and 5 centimeters dilated. My first reaction was, "What, I don't feel like I'm in labor!"(The nurse kindly enlightened me that the night my water broke, I was in labor!). Even though I was confident that she would be okay, apart of me was petrified because she was only 29 weeks. The other part was relieved to get freed from my hospital bed and that truth made me feel so guilty. I had to swallow all my fears and I put my "big girl panties" on because it was time to cross the finish line. It was time to get this baby here and I knew that God had the rest! The drama didn't stop there! Once the doctor checked me, she told me should could feel the feet dangling and instructed me to not bare down or push. They didn't want me to give birth vaginally because since my water broke nearly a month prior; I had little fluid and she was in a breeched position. The doctors instructed everyone to prep for my c-section and that wasn't hard to do because they were prepared nineteen days ago! My doctor grabbed my hand and told me she was so proud of me because only my strength and faith in God allowed me to hold that baby in so long. She told me that women usually deliver within two days of their water broking and that she had only seen one other case, where a woman was successful in putting her labor off. Even though I was disappointed that I couldn't lay longer; my heart rejoiced because I knew God granted me yet another miracle with allowing my baby to have more time to thrive in my womb. As quickly as the medical team was preparing, it felt like a lifetime to me. I lay in my hospital bed praying that I didn't give into the urge to push. Finally my bed began to roll down the hall towards the operating room. I was so delighted to see the world outside of my hospital room and window sill. But, apart of me was terrified of giving birth. I found myself in the coldness of the operating room, the medical staff's voices sound like noise; my fear had begin to tune everything out. My fog was lifted by, "Now, Mrs. Kinsey, I need you to turn on your right side and stay as still as you can, so that we can get the epidural in". Lord, I don't know where the strength came from but I bravely and immediately listened. I clinched my eyes shut to prepare for the pain. The numbing medicine went in first and it wasn't as bad as I thought. I spoke to soon because the staff had a problem with getting it in. I grew worried because five minutes turned to fifteen. I knew that if I was unable to get the epidural; that my husband couldn't be in the room with me because I would have to be fully sedated. The nurses and medical assistants were like family now; for God sakes, they wiped my butt everyday; so my comfort level with them was great! They held my hand and embraced my body, reassuring me it would be okay. But, to add to the drama, I was unable to sit up because my baby's feet were dangling and she had very little fluid around her. Then, the lightening struck and I heard the doctor yell frantically; "We have to fully sedate her now, I'm losing the baby's heartbeat, we have to go now". I felt paralyzed; my mind went to the absolute worst. I thought I lost my baby. By this time I could feel tears roll as I was slowly fading out because of the anesthesia. Before, I totally went under; a nurse grabbed my hand and said, "We found the heartbeat". I went off to sleep with relief.

I woke up to pain that was indescribable; but it was the price for waking up to my DESTINY. My daughter, Destiny Brielle Kinsey was born October 12, 2010 at 8:26am. It was the perfect time to end my journey of infertility and welcome the new one; motherhood. The road through infertility was over, but I knew that the recovery from the race was just beginning. But, for now

I just wanted to enjoy my victory with crossing the finish line; I'm sitting on the ground trying to catch my breath! I have the pleasure to regain my composure while nestling my baby. I finally met the girl of and in my dreams!

Love Letter to the Desiring Mother

Dear Mother,

I call you mother because that is exactly who you are. I believe you become a mother when your heart first conceives love and hope for your unborn baby. I write this letter to you in tears because I know the pain that you hold inside for not being able to nurture your own baby right at this present moment. I know how it feels to reach out for a dream that only seems to run forward instead of standing still so that you can grab it. I know your tears and as they roll down your face, my hands are open to catch them. Even though, I can not physically be there to wipe them away, they can rest inside the palms of my hands because as I clinch my hands to pray; I will send them to the Master. My heart is sensitive to your truth because I'm not that far removed from it. Even though my heart is big enough to love each of you and my arms can open wide enough to hug each of you, I've been sent to give a bigger message. That message is that God's love is much greater than me, you, and that baby that you pray so hard for. Despite the internal turmoil that infertility can bring; God's love for you is so much greater than it. It makes me emotional just to think how much he loves us. His affection and mercy towards us is immeasurable and so sweet. If you can't believe it because your pain is consuming you; look at my story and believe that the same God who turned my impossible to possible can do the same for you. If God could pull me from a place of death and stagnation; he can pull you out too. He wants to pull you out and he wants to give you what your heart desires. The same love that you hold in your heart for your wanted baby is the same love God has for you; his baby. You have to allow this process to teach you because I believe with everything in my heart that God had to take me through the test of infertility. The journey through infertility allowed for past hurt and trauma to surface; forcing me to deal with them and even though I still need deliverance from certain things; I have started the process. I am no longer afraid to stare my truth in the face and work towards a positive change. I'm not afraid to live through my struggles and appreciate the things that make up all of who I am. My prayer for you is to do the same thing, don't be afraid to live through your infertility. Don't be afraid to put it on the back burner, to focus on the things in your life that need a complete healing; so that you can carry on to the end of this journey. The times when you feel like you are residing inside your darkest hour, remember that God loves you and wants the very best for you. I know that it is hard to rationalize that because of the pain, but it is the truth. One thing that I can promise is that you will have that moment when peace will conquer everything. Peace will become your confidence and you will be able to run on to see what the end of this journey will bring. I thank you for allowing me and my words into your heart. I pray that you find solace and hope from the experiences that I faced. I know you because I am you and I know your pain because I had that pain. I will meet you on the other side of the finish line and we can sit together as we catch our breath to start the new JOURNEY . . . . But before I leave you I want to leave you with words from the great Tyler Perry that ignited a fire inside my soul. He said, (and I do paraphrase) "That it doesn't matter how many "No's" you get; you just need one "Yes" from God". That statement rings so precise and it takes me back to the entire No's" that I received in my journey to mother hood. The doctors, family, friends, and psychologists told me "No". But, God said "Yes" in spite of all hope being lost. And that in it self is the fuel that will drive you towards your journey's end . . . . I love you and wish you all the faith and success in your travels.

Yours Truly,
Dani

Love Letter to Destiny

Dear Destiny,

So much of my happiness starts with you; I only wish that you could know the person I was before so you can appreciate the person I am now; now that I have you. You are the reason why life is so beautiful; I swear I didn't appreciate the beauty of life until my ability to carry life was threatened. I fought so hard for you to be here and I refused to give up on you because I just knew you were waiting for me. For years I felt like you were calling my name and I just couldn't get to you. I was devastated at the prospect of never being able to see, hold, nurture, or answer your call. But, today I can touch you and every time I see your face, I'm reminded of God's mercy. I am reminded of his love towards me. Now, that you are here; I can't feel the crippling pain that once consumed me. All I feel is love towards you, my baby and my gift. For the rest of my life, I will strive to put my very best in you. And like any other good parent, I pray for the best for you and your brother. I want you to exceed expectations and be this phenomenal woman that I know you will be one day. I know you will succeed, because your name means just that and you have already proved that you are a fighter. Baby girl, I pray that you always keep that drive to fight through life. No, I'm not talking about physically fighting your way through life; but not allowing circumstances to weaken your drive and determination. We are both fighters, I have fought for everything I have and that's including you. So, my prayer is that we will always walk hand and hand together; fighting through life. Destiny, I love you more than these words can articulate, your presence has brought light back into my face. I wear a permanent smile because I know that you are mine. I am yours and I will be here for you, whenever you need me. I will be your best friend when everyone has left. I will be your confidant when there is no one to listen to you. I will be your protector when life wants to attack you. I will embrace you when you are scared and be your company when you are lonely. I will be your "voice of reason" when you are irrational and I will be your strength when you get too weak to fight. Destiny, I will have your back in any situation; right or wrong; bad or worse. You will never have to guess whose side I am on because I will always choose you; I am all yours. I am so excited to be in this life with you. All I want is to be the best woman I can be, so that you will have a great example to look up to. You make me want to be great and every time you smile at me; it gives me the motivation I need to be just that. I will be your mother forever, I will love you forever.

Loving you unconditionally,
Your Mother

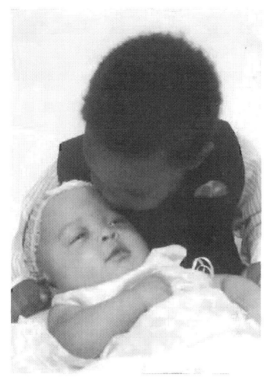

These tiny souls are my miracles! They are my reward
for my journey! My Destiny!

About the Author

Danielle Kinsey is a poet, blogger, writer, and educator who resides in Baltimore Maryland. She uses her poetry and personal experiences to express her raw emotions through her writing. Please visit her website, www. poeticphilosophy.com.